Famous African Americans Table

	Page	🌐	📖A	🔥	✍	🎨	✏	👕
About Famous African Americans	2							
Letter to Parents	4							
Letter to Students	5							
Assessment Test	6	•						
African Americans	8	•						
Black History Month	9	•						
Kwanzaa	10		•					
The Spingarn Medal	11		•					
The Underground Railroad	12	•						
Reading a Time Line	13	•			•			
Mary McLeod Bethune	14	••				•		
Gwendolyn Brooks	17	•	•				•	
George Washington Carver	20	•		•			•	•
Ray Charles	23	•				•	•	•
Bill Cosby	26		•	•				•
Gail Devers	29	•				•	•	•
Frederick Douglass	32		•		•		•	•
Charles Drew	35	•			•			•
Duke Ellington	38	•	•					
Matthew Henson	41	••					•	
Whitney Houston	44	•	••					
Michael Johnson	47	•			•		•	•
William Johnson	50	•				•	•	•
Michael Jordan	53	•	•				•	•
Jackie Joyner-Kersee	56	•			•		•	•
Martin Luther King, Jr.	59	••				•	•	•
Thurgood Marshall	62	••					•	•
Toni Morrison	65	••					•	
Colin Powell	68	•			•		•	•
Leontyne Price	71	•		•			•	•
David Robinson	74	•	••		•			
Wilma Rudolph	77	•				•	•	•
Harriet Tubman	80	••	•				•	
Booker T. Washington	83	•	•				•	•
Denzel Washington	86	••			•			
Daniel Hale Williams	89	•		•			•	•
Tiger Woods	92	•		•			•	•
Answer Key	95							

About *Famous African Americans*

This book relates historical events in the lives of 27 African Americans. The selections represent African-American achievements in music, science, politics, education, the arts, sports, medicine, civil rights, and the military. The biographical sketches relate not only the achievements of the individuals, but also the drive and effort necessary to accomplish them.

What You Will Find in This Book

- **Learning Assessment** to measure the students' progress for portfolios.
- **27 biographical events**
- **6 pages of general information** to enrich the students' understanding of African-American history and prepare them for some of the information they will encounter in the stories. These pages include **African Americans, Black History Month, Kwanzaa, the Spingarn Medal, the Underground Railroad,** and a **time line** which demonstrates the relationships between the people and some of the events that helped shape their lives.
- **Letters to parents and students**

The letter to the parents can be copied and sent home with the students. It will alert parents to be open to their children's questions about famous African Americans and will encourage discussion between parents and children. The letter to students is designed to encourage discussion and questions and to provoke interest about famous African Americans.

Organization

Each biographical event is part of a three-page section:

- **the story**,
- **a comprehension exercise and a critical thinking/writing exercise,**
- **a learning activity**

These activities encompass the curriculum areas of **social studies, language arts, science, math,** and **art.**

- **Icons** in the Table of Contents and next to each activity will help the teacher find curriculum-related activities.
- **Insets** on each story page either highlight a new fact or give more detail to the story.
- **Comprehension questions** test the students' understanding of what they've read.
- **Writing/critical thinking exercises** encourage students to think beyond their reading. The activities reinforce the learned materials in fun and interesting ways and sometimes introduce new, related materials.
- **Answer key** is on page 95.

Using *Famous African Americans*

Use this book as a tool to show students that people are more alike than different. We all hurt, love, feel fear, experience joy, and desire successes in our lives.

Many different careers are discussed in the biographies. Some may not be familiar to the students. Politics and the military, for example, will need to be discussed and explained before readers will understand what it means to run for an office or to serve in the Army. Class discussions about each career as it is encountered will enhance students' understanding of the people and their accomplishments.

Teachers may photocopy each of the lessons and have students secure them in a notebook or folder. The following activity suggestions provide opportunities to expand the lessons and to get the maximum benefit from this book. Some activities can be done individually, and others will lend themselves well to group or center activities.

Activity Suggestions

- Bring in newspaper/magazine articles about African Americans in the news. Share them with the class. Hang them on a special bulletin board. Pictures could be brought in of local people, including family.

- Have students write a letter to an African American who interests them.

- Invite local African-American achievers to come to the class and tell about their jobs (minister, businessperson, college professor, principal, construction worker, etc.).

- Have students make campaign signs, support for athlete signs, protest signs, etc., and mount them on sticks. Have students explain what they've done and why. (i.e., Colin Powell for President, Go Michael—Win the Championship for the Bulls, We Want Fair Treatment for African Americans, etc.).

- On a simple U.S. map, show students where each achiever lived, traveled, and worked.

- Use the time line to give students a clearer picture of when these people lived with respect to each other as well as in relation to what was happening in society at the time.

- Bring in recordings of Ray Charles, Whitney Houston, Leontyne Price, Duke Ellington, or Bill Cosby. Find and share samples of poetry or writing from Gwendolyn Brooks and Toni Morrison.

- As a follow-up activity for the unit, assign a famous African American to each student. Have each student use his or her book of biographies to write 2-3 clues to the identity of the assigned individual. Have the class guess the person's identity.

- Ask students to select an African-American achiever from their book and draw something that represents that person. The student can present the drawing to the class and have classmates guess the person's identity.

- Have students talk about how they could become famous Americans. For what would they like to be remembered? How do they plan to achieve their goals? Students should recognize that diligence, hard work, tenacity, integrity, commitment to a goal, and strong will are necessary elements for success.

Dear Parents,

To increase your child's understanding of our history and the contributions that African Americans have made, we will be studying 27 famous African Americans. The stories have been written with your child in mind. Each one centers on an important, interesting event. Two activity pages that complete each section will help your child remember his or her reading. They will also encourage your child to think beyond the story and to apply experiences to his or her own life. Your child may be assigned to bring these pages home for completion.

Regardless of whether these lessons are assigned as homework, please ask your child to talk about the stories. Share your own knowledge about famous African Americans. When your child sees that you are interested, it will spark his or her interest even more. If the pages are brought home for completion, please support your child by communicating your expectations that the work be done. You can provide this support by providing a quiet work area and by checking the work when your child has finished.

Since many of the lessons refer to exceptional effort on the part of the individual, you have an opportunity to talk with your child about those qualities which contribute to success in all fields of work. Identification of possible career interests emerges from these discussions.

Above all, enjoy this time with your child as together you learn more about famous African Americans.

Sincerely,

Dear Student:

You're about to have an adventure. You'll be amazed, surprised, and challenged. You're going to see what it takes to make a hero. You'll read about how hard it can be to change history, and then you'll see how rewarding it can be. You'll meet champions, winners, and people who worked quietly to make a big difference. You'll learn about people in science, sports, education, politics, the arts, and the armed forces. You'll learn about famous African Americans. You'll see how these incredible people made changes that improved the lives of not only African Americans, but of all Americans.

You will take a pre-test to show how much you already know about the famous African Americans that we will study. We will also study some background information to help you understand a few events which have helped shaped history. Then we will begin lessons of 27 famous African Americans.

Each of the lessons is a one-page story with two pages of activities. The activities give you an opportunity to apply what you have learned and to look at how the accomplishments of others affect you.

Please plan to keep all your lessons in a notebook or folder. You may want to decorate the folder! When you have done all the lessons, you will get to show how much you have learned. In order to help you remember the events and the people you will be studying, please talk about them with your family and friends.

Have fun as you begin this adventure. Plan to work hard and to learn everything you can!

Sincerely,

Name _____ Date _____

Make a Splash!

Show What YOU Know About Famous African Americans

Directions for 1-10: Circle the correct answer to complete each sentence.

1. Matthew Henson explored the _____ with Robert Peary.
   a. West **b.** North Pole **c.** Andes Mountains

2. Martin Luther King, Jr., is famous for his work in _____.
   a. education **b.** medicine **c.** civil rights

3. The _____ was a way for slaves to escape to freedom.
   a. Underground Railroad **b.** train **c.** Kwanzaa

4. Bill Cosby makes people ____ with his stories about everyday things.
   a. sad **b.** angry **c.** laugh

5. Mary McLeod Bethune started a _____ for African Americans.
   a. hospital **b.** school **c.** bank

6. _____ is the name of an African-American holiday.
   a. Kwanzaa **b.** Spingarn **c.** February

7. Colin Powell is a _____ and a military adviser.
   a. president **b.** war hero **c.** doctor

8. Whitney Houston and Leontyne Price are both famous for their ____ .
   a. singing **b.** writing **c.** artwork

9. Booker T. Washington was the founder of the _____ .
   a. Spingarn Medal **b.** North Pole **c.** Tuskegee Institute

10. Each year, the ____ is awarded to an outstanding African American.
    a. Nobel Prize **b.** Spingarn Medal **c.** Pulitzer Prize

Name _____ Date _____

Directions for 11-15: Fill in the blank with the correct answer.

11. _____ was called the Plant Doctor.

12. Two parts of the heptathalon are _____

    and _____ .

13. The event that brought the white and African-American people of

    Clarksville, Tennessee, together for the first time was_____

    _____ .

14. Dr. Charles Drew has helped millions of people through his work

    with _____ .

15. Michael Johnson and Gail Devers have _____ in common.

Directions for 16-18: Write a short sentence to answer each question.

16. What new way of writing did Toni Morrison use in *The Bluest Eye*?

    _____

17. Why did the Navy allow David Robinson to leave school early to

    play basketball? _____

    _____

18. What dangers did Harriet Tubman have to avoid when helping

    slaves escape to the free states? _____

    _____

    Why? _____

    _____

Name _____ Date _____

African Americans

African Americans are Americans who can say that someone in their family came from Africa. This person may have come to the United States over 100 years ago. It is possible that the person did not choose to come here. He or she may have come to the United States as a slave. There are about thirty million African Americans in America today.

African Americans have not had an easy life in the United States. For a long time, there were laws that told white people to treat African Americans differently. African Americans could not vote. They could not drink from the same water fountains as white people. Many restaurants would not serve them inside the building. They had to move to the back of a city bus if a white person wanted their seat.

Over time the laws were changed. Leaders like Dr. Martin Luther King, Jr., helped change them. Today there are laws that say all people must be treated the same, regardless of the color of their skin.

Your Family Tree

Family trees can go back many, many years. Here is a small one for you to fill in. You can write first names only.

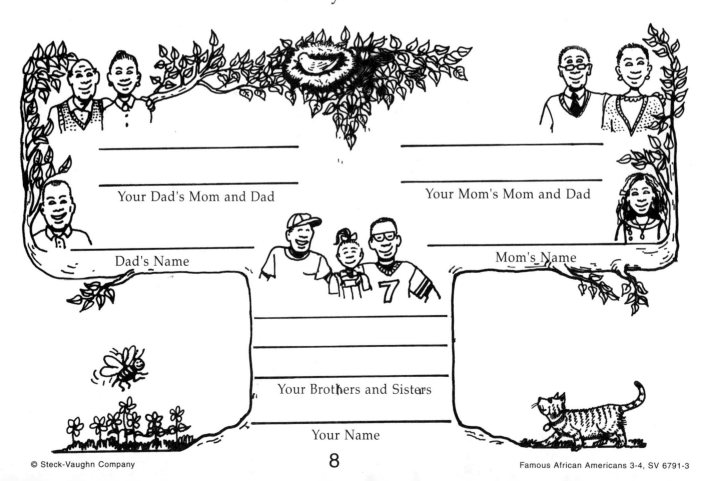

Name _____ Date _____

Black History Month
A Time to Celebrate African Americans

The month of February is Black History Month. It is a time when we learn more about African Americans who have done great things for our country.

Carter G. Woodson is called the Father of Black History. He started Negro History Week in 1926. He wanted people to honor the achievements of African Americans. Over the years this special time has become Black History Month.

Fill in the correct dates on the calendar below. (Note: This calendar has school days only—no weekends!) Each day that you learn about a different African American, write his or her name on your calendar. Write a couple of words to remind you of what that person did in his or her life.

FEBRUARY

Monday	Tuesday	Wednesday	Thursday	Friday

Name _____ Date _____

Kwanzaa
African-American Holiday

Kwanzaa is an African-American holiday. Kwanzaa means "first fruits." It is a way to end the old year and to start a new one. This holiday begins on December 26 and lasts for seven days.

Maulana Karenga (Mah-oo-LAN-nah Kar-REN-gah) started Kwanzaa in 1966. Now over 18 million people in the United States celebrate the holiday. It is a time for African Americans to think about their history and also their future.

On each day of Kwanzaa, people talk about one of the seven Kwanzaa ideas with their friends and family. Each day a different candle is lit. The candles are different colors: one black, three green, and three red. The black candle is lit the first night of Kwanzaa. The candles are put in a special holder called a kinara (kee-NAH-rah).

Cut out the seven candles below. On the back of each one, write what you could do to show the Kwanzaa idea. When you are finished, color the candles. Draw and cut out a kinara like the one on this page, and paste the ends of the candles on it.

1. I must work with others to get things done.

2. My name is _____ . I must be myself.

3. I am a helper. I need to help my family and community.

4. I need to help my friends.

5. I am responsible for what I do.

6. I am creative. I can do many things.

7. I believe in myself, my family, and my community.

Name _____ Date _____

The Spingarn Medal

The Spingarn Medal is given each year to an outstanding African American. It was Joel Spingarn's idea in 1914 to award this gold medal.

Many of the African Americans you will study have received the Spingarn Medal. These people had become the very best they could be at their profession.

To whom do you think the Spingarn Medal could go this year? Make a Spingarn Medal for him or her. Write why you think this person should get the award. Cut out the award, and be prepared to share it with the class.

Name _____ Date _____

The Underground Railroad
The Slaves' Path to Freedom

The Underground Railroad was not a real railroad. It was a way for slaves to escape to freedom. The runaway slaves had to travel at night and hide during the day. People who helped the slaves were called conductors. The conductors gave the slaves a hide-out, food, clothes, and money. The hiding places were called stations. From 1830 until 1860, thousands of slaves were able to escape with the help of the Underground Railroad.

Often the slaves went to the free states in Canada. They took many routes. Look at the old map below. Arrows show some of the routes the escaped slaves followed.

Slave States
Arkansas AK
Delaware DE
Kentucky KY
Maryland MD
Missouri MO
North Carolina NC
Tennessee TN
Virginia VA

Free States
Connecticut CT
Illinois IL
Indiana IN
Iowa IA
Kansas KS
Massachusetts MA
Maine ME
Michigan MI
Minnesota MN
New Hampshire NH
New Jersey NJ
New York NY
Ohio OH
Pennsylvania PA
Rhode Island RI
Vermont VT
Wisconsin WI

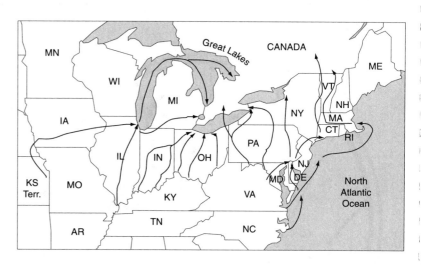

1. You are a slave in Kentucky. You want to go to Canada. Through which states could you travel?

_____ _____ _____

2. You will travel by boat from North Carolina to Delaware. On which ocean will you travel?

_____

3. Name 3 free states that had Underground Railroad routes in them.

_____ _____ _____

Name _____   Date _____

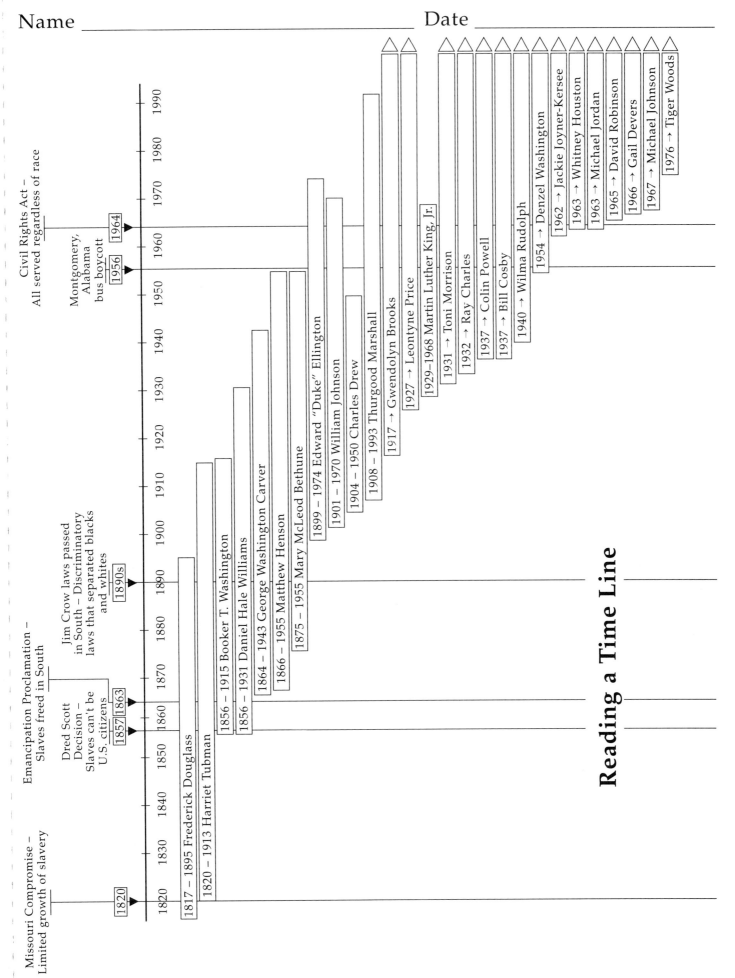

Reading a Time Line

Name _____ Date _____

Mary McLeod Bethune
Educator

It was the year 1907. Mary Bethune stood on the steps of her new school in Daytona Beach, Florida. Today she would welcome her first classes to Faith Hall. It was a happy day for her. She had worked hard to expand her school. As Mary watched her students arrive, she remembered how it had all begun.

"I'd like to buy a piece of property from you," Mary had told her landlord, Mr. Johnson. "I need more room for my school." The two went to look at some land. When they passed the trash dump, Mary said, "Stop, I want this land." Mr. Johnson tried to talk her out of buying it. Mary would not change her mind. "That is where my school will be," she told him. So Mr. Johnson agreed to sell the land for $250.

There was a problem. Mary didn't have any money. She had only a dream. Mary had a way of getting others to believe in her dreams. In one week she raised $15 for the down payment on the land. She promised to give Mr. Johnson more each month until the land was paid for. She would have to raise more money to do this.

Mary told everyone about her dream of a school for African-American children. Mary's dream became the dream of many people. Many who had money gave it to help Mary build her school. Others gave their time and hard work to help.

Over time Mary's school grew. Many new buildings were built near Faith Hall. Today the school is called Bethune-Cookman College. About 2,300 students attend the college every year.

Bethune Bits

Mary McLeod Bethune knew a lot about children and about education. Four United States Presidents asked Mary for her advice when they were making decisions about children and schools.

Mary was the first in her family to go to school. She walked five miles each way. She taught her family what she had learned.

Name _____ Date _____

What do you remember about Mary McLeod Bethune?

Circle the answer that best completes each sentence.

1. Mary's new school was called _____ .

   a. Harvard   b. Faith Hall   c. Bethune College

2. Mary opened her school in _____ .

   a. Texas   b. Kansas   c. Florida

3. _____ presidents of the United States asked Mary for help.

   a. All of the   b. Four   c. Two

4. Mary McLeod Bethune was the first in her family to _____ .

   a. go to school   b. drive   c. buy a house

5. Mary McLeod Bethune is remembered for bringing _____ to African Americans.

   a. food   b. education   c. music

More About Mary McLeod Bethune

In 1907 workers finished Mary's dream school. It was a four-story building. The floors were bare, and there weren't many windows. But Mary was very proud. She called her new school Faith Hall. Draw a picture of Faith Hall.

Name _____ Date _____

Building a School

Color these items you might find in an old schoolhouse. Cut them out. Then paste them into a shoe box to make a schoolroom.

Compare Mary Bethune's schoolroom with your schoolroom.
List the things that are the same and the things that are different.

Things That Are the Same	Things That Are Different

Gwendolyn Brooks
Poet

It was National Library Week in April of 1989. The crowd in Gary, Indiana, waited for their special guest. Children and adults paced about the warm meeting room. Gwendolyn Brooks was to arrive any minute.

They had all come to see the famous writer and poet, Gwendolyn Brooks. They wanted to meet the first African American who won the Pulitzer Prize. It is one of the best awards a writer can receive. Gwendolyn had won this award many years before, in 1950. She won it for her book of poems called *Annie Allen*. Since then Gwendolyn had written many other books of poetry.

The librarians had been waiting nearly an hour. They filled the time talking about Gwendolyn's poetry. Her poems, for children and adults, are about things people think, see, and feel. Gwendolyn has said that a writer must be able to see beauty where there is none. Then the writer must be able to describe the beauty for others to see and enjoy. The librarians agreed that Gwendolyn had followed her own advice about good writing. Her poetry describes life so everyone can enjoy it.

More About Gwendolyn Brooks

Gwendolyn's first poem was published when she was just 13 years old.

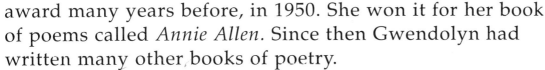

Soon there was a stir. Gwendolyn slipped in a side door and walked down the aisle. She was smiling broadly. People began to applaud as Gwendolyn went to the front of the room. She waited for the people to stop clapping and apologized for being late. "Believe me, I'll stay as long as you want me. I'll sign each slip of paper or book . . . " And she did. Her grace and good humor pleased those who had come to see her. It had been worth the wait to see this great writer.

Name _____ Date _____

What do you remember about Gwendolyn Brooks?

Read each sentence. Write *true* or *false* next to each one. If the story did not give you enough information to answer *true* or *false*, put a question mark in the blank.

_____ 1. Gwendolyn was a good writer.

_____ 2. Gwendolyn's first poem was published when she was nine years old.

_____ 3. Gwendolyn wrote poetry only for adults.

_____ 4. Gwendolyn's poetry appeared in magazines.

_____ 5. Gwendolyn won the Pulitzer Prize for her writing.

_____ 6. *Annie Allen* is Gwendolyn's only book of poetry.

_____ 7. Gwendolyn was the first African American to win the Pulitzer Prize.

More About Gwendolyn Brooks

Gwendolyn Brooks has written many poems. Poetry often uses words that rhyme. Write three words that rhyme with each of the words below.

1. sent

_____ _____ _____

2. charm

_____ _____ _____

3. slip

_____ _____ _____

4. books

_____ _____ _____

Name _____ Date _____

Writing a Poem

Read this poem by Larry Hodge.

A Friend Is . . .

A friend is a rock that never crumbles,
A cloud that never rains,
A mount that never stumbles,
A bond that still remains.

A friend is a road that never ends,
A river that runs so deep,
A tree that never bends,
A treasure meant to keep.

A friend is a gift myself I give,
A prize I hope I win,
A safe place that I can live,
A guest I welcome in.

A friend is my own perfect self,
A person I'd like to be,
A trophy sitting on a shelf,
A mirror reflecting me.

Larry Hodge

Did you enjoy reading this poem? Hodge could have written, "Friends are great!" But he wrote a poem instead. The poem is fun to read and makes us think about how it feels to have friends.

In many poems the sentences end with rhyming words. Circle the rhyming words in Hodge's poem.

Write your own poem. First, think about what you will write. What are some words you could use that will rhyme? Share your poem.

Name _____ Date _____

George Washington Carver
Plant Doctor

"Dr. Carver, what will we do with all these peanuts?" one farmer asked. "How will we make money to feed our families?" another said. It was the early 1900s. Dr. George Washington Carver knew the farmers were right. Earlier they had come to him for help. They were having trouble with their cotton crops. He had told them to plant peanuts instead of cotton. Many farmers did as he said. Now they had more peanuts than they could sell. Dr. Carver had to help the farmers find a way to sell their crops of peanuts.

He went to work in his lab at the Tuskegee Institute in Alabama. For days he mashed and ground peanuts. He added water. He froze them. He tried many different ways to use peanuts. At last Dr. Carver could help the farmers. He had found over 300 ways to use peanuts.

Dr. Carver showed the farmers some of the products he made with the peanuts. He showed them milk, shampoo, face powder, ink, coffee, and soap. The farmers couldn't believe their eyes. They wanted to taste the food. Others wanted to use the ink.

Word soon spread about Dr. Carver's peanut products. Now everyone wanted peanuts. People came from other states. The farmers were able to sell their crops. Dr. Carver had again helped the southern farmers.

More on Dr. Carver

Dr. Carver could have made a lot of money from his ideas, but he shared them for free. He also gave most of his money back to the Tuskegee Institute. He wanted other people to keep on with his work. He is remembered as a great scientist.

Name _____ Date _____

What do you remember about George Washington Carver?

Choose the best ending for each sentence. Fill in the circle next to it.

1. George Washington Carver was known as the
   - ○ a. family doctor.
   - ○ b. plant doctor.
   - ○ c. animal doctor.
   - ○ d. none of the above
2. Dr. Carver worked
   - ○ a. at the Tuskegee Institute.
   - ○ b. at the San Diego Zoo.
   - ○ c. with the southern farmers.
   - ○ d. both at the Tuskegee Institute and with the southern farmers.
3. Dr. Carver used peanuts
   - ○ a. only one way.
   - ○ b. just under 20 ways.
   - ○ c. over 300 ways.
   - ○ d. none of the above
4. Dr. Carver is remembered as a great
   - ○ a. teacher.
   - ○ b. farmer.
   - ○ c. scientist.
   - ○ d. all of the above.

More About George Washington Carver

Dr. Carver used peanuts in making soap, flour, ink, paint, cream, coffee, and many other things. Choose something made from peanuts. Pretend you are selling it. Write some sentences telling why people should buy it.

_____

_____

_____

_____

Name _____   Date _____

Growing a Plant

George Washington Carver found that many things could be made from peanuts. Peanuts come from a bush that grows above the ground. But the peanut pods grow under the ground. The growing stages of a peanut plant are as follows:

1. The plant, or bush, has flowers that die and fall off.

2. The stems that the flowers leave behind grow toward the ground.

3. The stems, called pegs, push into the dirt.

4. The pegs get bigger underground and grow into peanut pods.

Look at the drawings of the stages of a peanut plant. Put a number, from 1 to 4, in each circle to show the correct order. Color the pictures, cut them out, and place them in the correct order for a book.

• You can grow a plant in your classroom. All you need is a small plastic bag, a lima bean seed, a damp paper towel, and a piece of tape. Put a seed in your bag. Add the paper towel. Close the bag and tape it to a sunny window. In a few days, your seed will begin to grow, and you'll be able to watch it!

Ray Charles
Musician

Imagine that you cannot see. You have to depend on your other senses to know what is going on around you. Your sense of hearing is keen. The smells in the air tell you everything. Your taste buds are alive in your mouth. Your hands see for you when you touch the things you use every day.

Now imagine that, although you cannot see, you can make wonderful music. You can play the piano and the saxophone. When you sing your songs, your voice is full of soul. People the world over know your music. They buy your jazz records and come from miles away to hear you perform.

Imagine that you are Ray Charles. Ray has been unable to see since he was a six-year-old in Georgia. He began piano lessons soon afterward at a Florida school for people who are blind. By the time he was 15, he was playing in clubs. At 17 he formed a trio, and at 22 he had a rhythm and blues group.

Ray has become a respected and loved jazz musician. His smile and his voice are hard to resist. People of all ages enjoy his musical style. Ray may not be able to see, but he brings light wherever he plays.

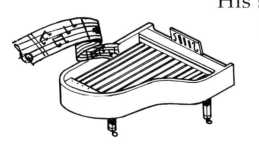

Writing Ray

Ray Charles is not only a great musician. He has written over 500 songs!

Name _____ Date _____

What do you remember about Ray Charles?

Read each sentence. Circle the word that best completes the sentence. Then write the word on the line.

1. Ray Charles is a popular _____ .

      artist   **musician**

2. Ray's music is full of _____ .

      soul   **mistakes**

3. Ray Charles has written about _____ songs.

      500   **55**

4. People all over the _____ enjoy Ray Charles' music.

      world   **city**

5. Ray Charles has been _____ since he was a young boy.

      sad   **unable to see**

More About Ray Charles

A man named Mr. Pit took an interest in Ray when he was three years old. He taught Ray how to play simple songs on the piano. Mr. Pit was an important person in Ray's childhood.

Write about a person who is important to you. What has this person taught you?

_____

_____

_____

_____

© Steck-Vaughn Company   Famous African Americans 3–4, SV 6791-3

Name _____ Date _____

Putting Together a Puzzle

Ray Charles often writes songs, sings them, and plays the piano. Cut out the puzzle pieces and put them together to find out another musical instrument Ray Charles plays.

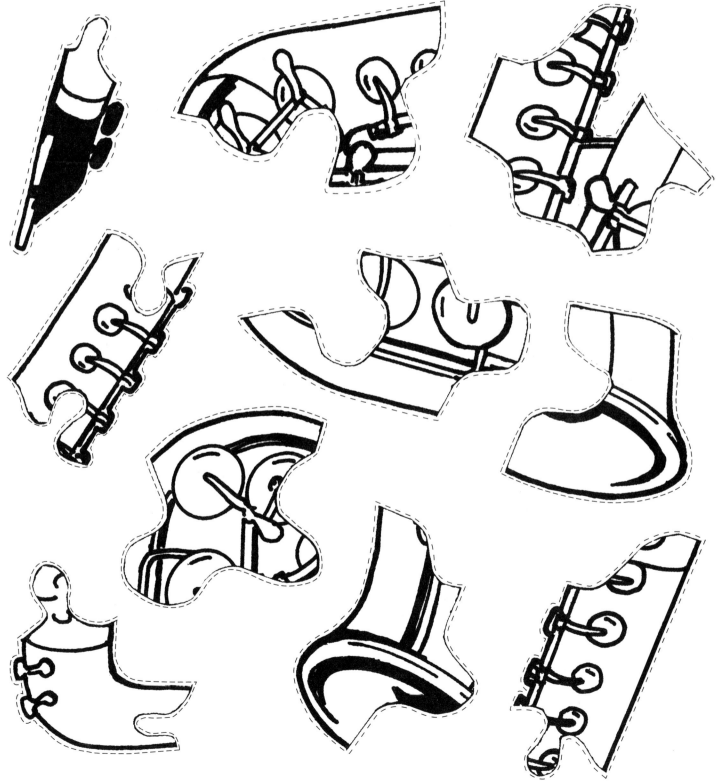

Name _____ Date _____

Bill Cosby
Comedian/Actor

A murmur goes through the audience at a club in Philadelphia. The act they came to see is late. They are getting restless. Then the owner of the club speaks into the microphone. He says the original act for tonight has been canceled. Instead, he introduces a new young comedian. His name is Bill Cosby.

Some of the people in the audience know Bill. He works in the club! He's pretty funny, sure, but can he do an act? Some people don't know Bill at all. They didn't come to see some new act.

By the time Bill Cosby is through, everyone is happy. The audience loves him. Their sides ache from laughing. The club owner has a new act. He knows people will come back to see Bill. And Bill has a new career. It is the early 1960s. Bill Cosby is soon to become one of America's best-known and best-loved comedians.

Bill Cosby has been making America laugh for years. Since he started in clubs, he has found many other ways to reach his audience. We listen to his records. We watch him on television. We see him in movies, and we read his books.

Bill isn't always doing a comedy act. But whatever he does, his gentle humor shows through. He makes us laugh at everyday things. Without being mean or picking on people, Bill Cosby shows us the humor in life.

Way to Go, Bill!

Bill had dropped out of college to be a full-time comedian. Later he went back to graduate. He then went on to get a master's degree and a doctorate in education from the University of Massachusetts!

Name _____ Date _____

What do you remember about Bill Cosby?

Underline the true sentence about Bill Cosby in each group.

1. a. Bill left college to live with his brother.
   b. Bill left college to join the Navy.
   c. Bill left college to be a comedian.

2. a. Bill got his first big break in television.
   b. Bill's first big break came when he was working in a club.
   c. Bill's first big break came while he was in the Navy.

3. a. Bill Cosby is a magician.
   b. Bill Cosby writes music.
   c. Bill Cosby is a comedian.

4. a. Bill's jokes make us laugh about life.
   b. Bill's jokes make us laugh at other people.
   c. Bill's jokes make us feel funny.

5. a. Bill Cosby's jokes are funny for all people.
   b. Bill Cosby's jokes are about white people.
   c. Bill Cosby's jokes are for African Americans only.

More About Bill Cosby

Bill Cosby tells jokes and funny stories about family life. Think of your favorite funny story about your family. Write it to share with the class.

_____

_____

_____

_____

Name _____ Date _____

Making a Puppet

Bill Cosby has a talent for telling stories that make people laugh. Bill's jokes make us laugh at life and at ourselves, not at other people.

Color the puppet of Bill Cosby. When you finish, cut it out. Tape it to a pencil. Use your puppet, and tell a funny story or joke to a friend.

Name _____ Date _____

Gail Devers
Olympic Runner

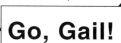

In 1992 the Olympic Games were in Barcelona, Spain. Gail Devers stood ready on the track. She was one of the eight fastest women in the world. Soon the 100-meter dash would begin.

Four years earlier Gail was well on her way to the Olympics in Seoul. She had been training hard. She was ready to run the 100-meter hurdles. Her coach, Bobby Kersee, had helped her believe in herself. Gail was a winner, and he knew it.

What happened next was a mystery. Gail began to feel sick. She could not run well. She was tired and weak. Doctors could not figure out what was wrong with her. Finally they found she had a rare illness called Graves' Disease. Her first treatment made her even sicker. The doctors thought they might have to operate to remove Gail's feet.

But one of her doctors changed her treatment, and Gail began to get better. As soon as she could walk, she was on the track again. At first she wore only socks. Later she put on her track shoes and began running. She began to train for Barcelona.

In Barcelona the race began. Eight women sprinted from the starting blocks. Just a year and a half after thinking she might never walk again, Gail Devers flew across the finish line. She had won the gold for the 100-meter dash.

Gail says being sick was very tough, but it made her a stronger person. "After conquering Graves' Disease, I know there's no hurdle I can't get over."

Go, Gail!

Gail's high school in National City, California, had no track team and no coach. She practiced alone. She was the only one on her team at track meets. Still, she won many races.

Gail still takes medicine for Graves' Disease. She is careful of what she eats and gets plenty of rest.

Name _____ Date _____

What do you remember about Gail Devers?

Write words from the box to answer the questions below. You will not use all the words from the box.

practice	run	100-meter dash
Barcelona, Spain	National City, California	hurdles
Seoul, Korea	swimming	Atlanta, Georgia

1. Where did Gail Devers go to high school?

   _____

2. What did Gail have to do alone in high school?

   _____

3. In which events did Gail run?

   _____

4. From your reading, in which Olympics did Gail win the 100-meter dash?

   _____

5. Bonus: Gail won the gold for the 100-meter dash in the 1996 Summer Olympics, too. Where were these Olympics?

   _____

More About Gail Devers

In school Gail liked helping other students. She thought she might like to be a teacher. What has Gail taught you? Write about it.

_____

_____

_____

Name _____ Date _____

Putting on a Play

You could be a playwright! Think about what happened in the story about Gail Devers. How would you put on a play to describe the events?

1. How many actors or actresses would you need to tell the story? Choose classmates to play each part.
   a. Gail Devers _____
   b. Coach Bobby Kersee _____
   c. Doctor #1 _____
   d. Doctor #2 _____
   e. Other _____

2. What will your actors and actresses need to wear to make them look like the person they are playing?
   a. Gail Devers _____
   b. Coach Bobby Kersee _____
   c. Doctor #1 _____
   d. Doctor #2 _____
   e. Other _____

3. What kinds of props, or items needed to tell your story, will you use? For example, a doctor may want to hold a clipboard.
   a. Gail Devers _____
   b. Coach Bobby Kersee _____
   c. Doctor #1 _____
   d. Doctor #2 _____
   e. Other _____

4. Think about what your actors and actresses might say to each other. Write their parts on another sheet of paper.

Extra: As a small group, practice your play. Present it to the class!

Frederick Douglass
Fighter for Freedom

On January 1, 1863, several thousand people against slavery met in Tremont Temple in Boston, Massachusetts. Both white and African-American people were there. They were waiting for the news of the Emancipation Proclamation that would free all slaves. It was expected any minute. President Lincoln had promised January 1 would be the day. But now it was close to nightfall. Where was the messenger with the news?

Frederick Douglass was in the crowd. He gave many speeches that night. Frederick had been a slave years ago. But he had escaped and later bought his freedom from his owner. He taught himself to read and write, and he became a well-known speaker. He shared his experiences as a slave with many people. He convinced many people slavery was wrong. He also wrote a newspaper, *The North Star*, that many African Americans and white people read. It contained more about his life as a slave.

Time seemed to go by slowly as everyone in the hall waited. Finally, at 10:00 that night, a messenger burst into the Temple yelling, "It is coming! It is on the wires!" Shouts, cheers, and tears of joy filled the hall. The slaves were freed! Soon thousands of happy voices were raised in song. Celebrations continued throughout the night.

The news of the Emancipation Proclamation must have been especially sweet for Frederick Douglass. Since his own escape, he had done everything he could to help other slaves become free. He had rarely stopped working for what he believed. His name became a symbol of freedom among all people.

Frederick's Story

After Frederick escaped, he changed his name so that his owner could not find him. But later, he wrote a book in which he named his owner. His owner came after him, but Frederick escaped to England. Still later, with the help of friends, he was able to buy his freedom.

Name _____ Date _____

What do you remember about Frederick Douglass?

Read the sentences about Frederick Douglass. Then write them in order to tell the story of Frederick's life.

Frederick bought his freedom from his owner.
Frederick ran away to freedom.
Frederick told people of his experiences as a slave.
Frederick wrote a book and printed a newspaper.
President Lincoln ordered the Emancipation Proclamation.

1. _____

2. _____

3. _____

4. _____

5. _____

More About Frederick Douglass

After Frederick wrote his book, his owner tried to find him. Frederick went to England. His friends there helped him get the money to buy his freedom. They also gave him money to help free other slaves. How do you think Frederick felt about his friends? Write what you think.

_____

_____

Name _____ Date _____

Breaking the Secret Code

Read the question. To break the code, write the first letter of each object in the box above it. When you are finished, you will know the answer to the question.

Question: What helped guide slaves to the free states?

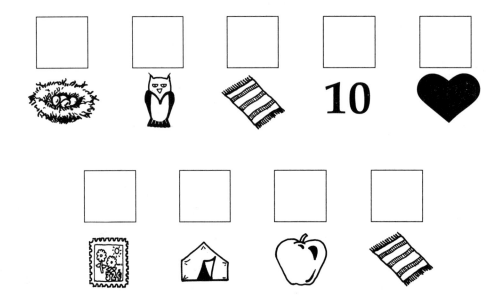

Name _____ Date _____

Charles Richard Drew
Scientist

It was 1940. World War II raged in Europe. In England soldiers lay in hospital beds near death. They had been wounded and needed blood. In America Dr. Charles Drew held an emergency cablegram in his hands. "We need ten thousand pints of plasma shipped within one month," Dr. Beattie from England pleaded. Dr. Drew knew he could help save some of these soldiers.

Dr. Drew was an African-American surgeon known for his study of blood. He discovered a way to take blood from one person and save it. Later the same blood could be given to someone else who needed it. This is a difficult task. Blood can be stored for only one week before it spoils. Dr. Drew discovered that blood plasma would keep much longer. Blood plasma is the liquid part of the blood without the blood cells. In the 1930s and before, many patients died because blood of the right type and match could not be found quickly enough. It often spoiled before it could be used.

The soldiers in England were lucky. They were given a chance to live because of Dr. Drew's system of storing blood plasma. Dr. Drew gathered the blood needed. He shipped it to Dr. Beattie to give to the soldiers. Many of them lived and went home to their families.

Later Dr. Drew worked with the Red Cross in the United States. With them he helped set up a blood program for the U.S. We still use Dr. Drew's system of storing blood today.

More on Charles Drew

At his high school in Washington D.C., Charles Drew was a star in football, basketball, baseball, and track. He was an all-American football player in college. Before he developed his interest in medicine, he was an athletic director in Maryland.

Name _____ Date _____

What do you remember about Dr. Charles Richard Drew?

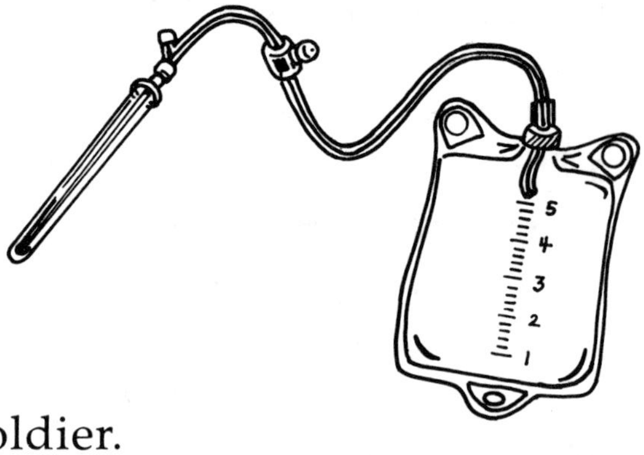

Read each of the sentences below. Underline the sentences that are not correct. Rewrite them so that they are true.

1. Charles Drew was a well-known soldier.

   _____

2. Dr. Drew thought of a way to save blood longer.

   _____

3. The Red Cross Blood Bank kept Dr. Drew's money.

   _____

4. Dr. Drew's system for storing blood is no longer used today.

   _____

5. Dr. Drew's blood system helped save many lives in World War II.

   _____

More About Charles Richard Drew

Dr. Charles Drew enjoyed helping other people. List three ways you can help other people.

1. _____
2. _____
3. _____

Name _____ Date _____

Using a Graph

Dr. Charles Richard Drew is remembered for his study of blood. You can find out something about blood, too.

- An adult who weighs 160 pounds has about 5 quarts, or 10 pints, of blood in his or her body. A child who weighs 80 pounds has about $2\frac{1}{2}$ quarts, or 5 pints, of blood.

Follow these steps to estimate how much blood you have in your body:

1. Write your weight. _____

2. Find your weight on the chart.

3. Draw a line straight across from your weight until you reach the bar that shows how much blood you have. Write your answer.

_____

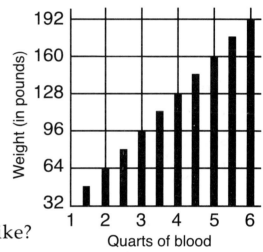

Measuring

- How much is a pint? What does a quart look like?

1. Get a cup, a pint, a quart, and a gallon container you can use to measure water.

2. How many cups will fit into a pint? _____

3. How many pints will fit into a quart? _____

4. How many cups will fit into a quart? _____

5. How many quarts will fit into a gallon? _____

6. Get a large bucket. Pour water into the bucket to equal the amount of blood you have in your body. Did you know your body held this much liquid?

7. If your teacher filled the bucket with enough water to equal the amount of blood in his or her body, would there be more or less water than there was when you filled the bucket for yourself? _____

Name _____ Date _____

Edward "Duke" Ellington
Jazz Musician

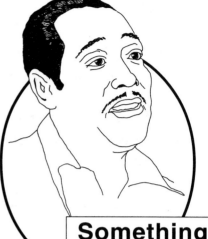

"Happy birthday, dear Duke, happy birthday to you," the guests all sang. Everyone was smiling at Duke Ellington. This night in 1969 was his night. It was his seventieth birthday. The President of the United States was giving him a birthday party at the White House in Washington D.C., Duke's birthplace. Over a hundred people were there to honor him.

Duke Ellington was a famous musician. He was the first to play long pieces of jazz music. He was also the first to perform jazz often. He and his famous band made jazz well-known and loved.

After dinner President Nixon asked the guests to come to the East Room. There he gave Duke a very special present. It was the Medal of Freedom. This award is the highest award the government can give a citizen. The President said, "In ... American music, no man ... stands higher than the Duke." Duke was very proud. Later he played a special song on the piano for the guests.

The party ended about two o'clock in the morning. Back at his hotel, Duke changed into his travel clothes. He stuffed his birthday cards into his coat pockets before he left. He had a plane to catch. Sleep would have to wait. Duke Ellington, the seventy-year-old jazz musician, had a concert to give the next night!

Something to Remember

Duke Ellington is famous for the music he wrote. He is also famous as a jazz band leader. In his band, the Cotton Club Orchestra, there were many famous musicians.

Duke got his name when he was a young boy. People noticed what a snappy dresser he was. The name stayed with him when he grew up.

Name _____ Date _____

What do you remember about Duke Ellington?

Find the best ending for each sentence.
Fill in the circle next to it.

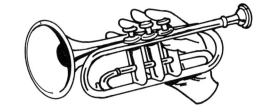

1. Edward Ellington was given the name "Duke" because he
   - ○ a. had fine manners and dressed well.
   - ○ b. worked for a king.
   - ○ c. lived in England.

2. Duke's jazz band was called
   - ○ a. the Dukes.
   - ○ b. the Jazz Club Band.
   - ○ c. the Cotton Club Orchestra.

3. Duke Ellington wrote
   - ○ a. TV shows.
   - ○ b. 2,000 letters.
   - ○ c. many songs.

4. The President of the United States gave Duke
   - ○ a. the Presidential Medal of Freedom.
   - ○ b. a job at the White House.
   - ○ c. a new piano.

5. Duke Ellington wrote and performed music and lead a
   - ○ a. parade.
   - ○ b. band.
   - ○ c. fox hunt.

More about Duke Ellington

Duke Ellington's style of music was known as jazz. Can you think of other kinds of music? Write three of them.

1. _____

2. _____

3. _____

Name _____ Date _____

Writing a Song

Writing new music the way Duke Ellington did is hard work. But you can give an old song new words to make it different. Each of the boxes below has different kinds of words. For example, Box 1 has words that are nouns. Box 2 has words that are verbs. Box 3 has words that are adjectives. Box 4 also has nouns.

Fill in the following blanks using your name and the words from the box number below each line. When you are finished, sing your new song to the tune of "Mary Had a Little Lamb." Try it with other words from the boxes. Your song may make sense, or it may be silly.

Box 1	Box 2	Box 3	Box 4
dog	run	curly	hair
cat	swim	shaggy	eyes
turtle	crawl	pointed	legs
cow	jump	round	fur
fish	sleep	slippery	scales

_____ had a little _____ ,
      (your name)   (Box 1)

Little _____ , little _____ .
    (same from Box 1)   (same from Box 1)

_____ had a little _____ who
      (your name)   (same from Box 1)

could _____ and had _____
        (Box 2)   (Box 3)

_____ .
       (Box 4)

Matthew Henson
Polar Explorer

It was 25 degrees below zero. The men could hardly breathe. The cold air burned their lungs. Ice coated their beards. For 18 years they had tried to reach this place. The day was April 6, 1909. Matthew Henson and Robert Peary were on top of the world. They were the first explorers to reach the North Pole.

The men looked around them. All they could see was a blanket of snow and ice. Robert said, "This scene my eyes will never see again. Plant the Stars and Stripes over there, Matt, at the North Pole."

Robert gave Matthew the flag. Robert had kept the flag under his shirt. It was wrapped around his body next to his skin. The cold wind whipped the flag open. The red, white, and blue colors were bright against the snow. Matthew Henson put the flag into the ground. Both men proudly watched the flag ripple in the wind.

Matthew Henson and Robert Peary were brave explorers. They never gave up. Many times they almost starved to death on their trips. Other times they nearly died in blizzards. But they both wanted to be the first explorers to reach the North Pole. They worked together to reach their goal. Matthew and Robert brought honor to the United States of America.

Discover More about Matthew Henson

The Inuits of the North taught Matthew many things about living in the cold. He learned how to handle a dog team. He learned how to hunt seal and bear for food and clothing. The Inuits also taught Matthew their language.

Name _____ Date _____

What do you remember about Matthew Henson?

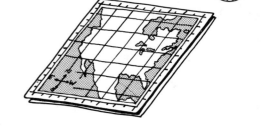

Underline the word or group of words that best completes each sentence.

1. Matthew traveled with the explorer, _____ .
   a. Robert Hope
   b. Ponce de Leon
   c. Robert Peary

2. _____ taught Matthew Henson to hunt seal and bear.
   a. Robert Peary
   b. African Americans
   c. Inuits

3. Matthew and Robert arrived at the _____ in 1909.
   a. North Pole
   b. Olympics
   c. state of Alaska

4. Matthew Henson planted _____ at the North Pole.
   a. his feet
   b. the American flag
   c. beans

5. Matthew and Robert started their journeys to the North Pole in _____ .
   a. 1891
   b. 1901
   c. 1801

More About Matthew Henson

For many years Matthew Henson and Robert Peary explored new places. Think of the last place you explored. Was it an old barn or a new house? Was it a museum? Or was it a hiking trail? Write about it. Be prepared to tell your classmates about it.

_____

_____

Name _____ Date _____

Making a Map

When Matthew Henson and Robert Peary explored new places, Robert made maps. Maps use pictures, or symbols, to tell about places. Imagine that you have just found a new place. Does it have many mountains, or is it flat? Does it have a lake or river, or is it dry? Use the symbols on the map key below. Make your own symbols if you need more.

Draw the symbols to make a map of your discovery.

 =Lake   = Mountains   = Forest    = River

Whitney Houston
Singer/Actress

The lights dimmed. A hush fell over the crowd. The men wore tuxedos, and the women were dressed in beautiful gowns. Many of them were famous singers, actors, and actresses. A woman came on stage. The crowd clapped and became quiet again. They wanted to hear the singer who had taken the music world by storm.

The place was Los Angeles. The woman was Whitney Houston. And she was singing at the twenty-first annual American Music Awards. The date was February 7, 1994. By the end of that night, Whitney would be given seven honors. She would also be given the Award of Merit for "outstanding contributions to the music and entertainment" of Americans.

Twelve years earlier Whitney was just 19 years old. She signed a contract to make a record. She was ready to wait years to become well-known. That day she only wanted to make a record. That record, *Whitney Houston*, turned out to be the all-time best-selling first record for a single singer.

From that time on, Whitney's success only grew. She made more records and began to make movies. Sometimes it was hard for Whitney to handle being so famous so fast. But her family is very close. They helped her through those times.

Whitney has loved singing since she was a child in New Jersey. Her message to America is, "Tell 'em that Whitney Houston still loves entertaining as much as she did when she was 19. And she probably still will when she's 99."

What else, Whitney?

Whitney starred with Kevin Costner in *The Bodyguard*, her first movie.

The music from that movie helped her to be named the "number one world artist" in 1993. She also won 11 trophies for those songs.

Name _____ Date _____

What do you remember about Whitney Houston?

Read the sentences below. Choose the correct answer. Write it in the blank.

1. Whitney Houston is from _____ .

   Maine **California** **New Jersey**

2. Whitney's first movie was called _____ .

   Whitney Houston *The Bodyguard* *Waiting to Exhale*

3. Whitney signed a record _____ when she was 19 years old.

   label **album** **contract**

4. The _____ from *The Bodyguard* did even better than the movie.

   music **actors** **popcorn sales**

5. Whitney's _____ helped her deal with being famous.

   money **sense of humor** **family**

More About Whitney Houston

Whitney's mother was a singer. Whitney loved to listen to her. She learned much about how to sing from her mother. Think of a skill you have learned by watching someone in your family. Write about it.

_____

_____

_____

© Steck-Vaughn Company   45   Famous African Americans 3-4, SV 6791-3

Name _____ Date _____

Breaking the Code

Find out the names of two of Whitney's most famous songs.

Look at Song Number One. Each space has a picture below it. Write the letter that begins the name of the picture in the blank. Continue until all the blanks are filled. Do the same with Song Number Two.

Song Number One:

"___ ___ ___   ___ ___ ___ ___ ___ ___ ___ ___

___ ___ ___ ___   ___ ___   ___ ___ ___"
    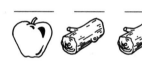

Song Number Two:

"___ ___ ___ ___ ___   ___ ___ ___ ___ ___ ___

___ ___ ___ ___   ___ ___ ___"

Michael Johnson
Olympic Athlete

"Michael, Michael, Michael," the crowd chanted. They had come from all over the world to Atlanta, Georgia, for the 1996 Summer Olympics. Standing in lane three, in golden shoes, was the man they had come to see.

Michael Johnson paced on the track. He had already won first place in the 400-meter race. Now he was trying for the gold medal in the 200-meter race. No man had ever won both races in the Olympics. Michael Johnson stood on the edge of history.

The starter called the racers to their lanes. Michael dropped to one knee. He placed his feet in the blocks. As he looked down the track, he focused on his goal. Years of practice had brought him to this moment in time. The starting gun fired. Michael exploded out of the blocks.

In Atlanta time seemed to stop. Eight of the world's fastest men sped around the track. Legs kicked. Arms pumped. Michael was a blur as he burst across the finish line. A giant timer showed the world the news. The gold medal was his in record-shattering time. Michael Johnson was the fastest man in the world. He (and his shoes) were as good as gold.

Later Michael said, "I'd never seen a crowd like this. The crowd really helped me. They deserve the world record."

More on Michael

Michael Johnson grew up near Dallas, Texas. He says his heroes were never athletes. His role model was his father.

Name _____ Date _____

What do you remember about Michael Johnson?

 Read each sentence. Circle the word or group of words that best completes the sentence. Then write the word or words on the line.

1. Michael Johnson is a champion _____ .

    runner   **swimmer**

2. Everyone noticed the special _____ Michael wore at the Olympic Games in Atlanta.

    running shorts   **shoes**

3. Michael Johnson was the first man to win both the _____ -meter and the 400-meter races in an Olympics.

    600   **200**

4. Michael Johnson ran the _____ -meter race faster than any man has ever run it.

    200   **400**

5. Michael Johnson is the _____ man alive.

    strongest   **fastest**

More About Michael Johnson

Athletes and rock stars were never Michael's heroes. Instead, his role model was his father. Think of someone you look up to. Why is that person important to you? Write about that person.

_____

_____

_____

_____

Name _____ Date _____

Measuring in Meters

Michael Johnson is known for his speed in the 200- and 400-meter races. Races in track are measured in meters instead of yards. A meter is about 39 inches long. Cut out the rulers below. Tape them together to make a ruler 39 inches, one meter, long.

Measuring:

1. Use your meter ruler to measure how tall you are. Write your height in meters. _____

2. How long is your classroom from front to back? _____

Estimating:

1. Estimate the length of your cafeteria in meters. _____

2. Guess how many meters make the length of a football field. _____

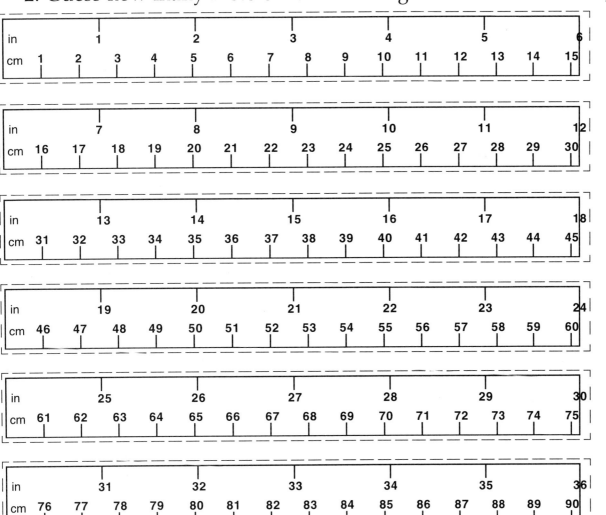

49

William H. Johnson
Artist

In New York in 1992, two art exhibitions were held. Many people came and admired the paintings there. They showed rough, powerful forms and bright, vivid colors. The people in the paintings were African Americans. There were pictures of Harlem and scenes from the painter's childhood in South Carolina.

The painter, William Henry Johnson, had waited a long time for America to take interest in his work.

William was born in 1901 in South Carolina. When he was 17, he went to New York City to study art. He worked for three years until at last he got into the National Academy of Design. William then studied art under the painter George Hawthorne. Hawthorne gave him money to go to Paris, France. William tried many different types of art and had his first art show in Paris. Back in America in 1930, he won a contest in New York. But, as an African-American artist, he did not feel accepted in America. He soon returned to Europe.

William finally found his own painting style when he visited Tunisia in Africa. He began painting folk art with strong shapes and bright colors. He began to paint the pictures of African Americans for which he would be remembered.

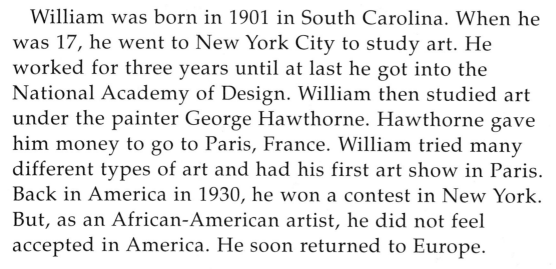

When William's work was shown in New York, he had been dead for 22 years. But, at last, Americans have found the beauty in his work, and William has found his place in American art.

William's Work

While waiting to get into art school in New York, William had many different jobs. In hotels he carried the guests' bags and cooked. On the docks William helped load ships.

Name _____ Date _____

What do you remember about William Johnson?

Write *true* or *false* on the line before each sentence. If the story did not give you enough information to answer the question, put a question mark in the blank.

_____ 1. William Henry Johnson was born in Maryland.

_____ 2. George Hawthorne wished he could go to Paris.

_____ 3. William tried many types of art.

_____ 4. William began to paint folk art in Africa.

_____ 5. William always wanted to live in California.

_____ 6. William painted pictures of African Americans.

_____ 7. Americans have never seen William Johnson's paintings.

More About William Johnson

William tried many different ways of painting before he found the way he liked best.

Think of something you have tried in different ways. What was not good about the first way you tried? What do you like about the way you do it now?

_____

_____

_____

_____

Name _____ Date _____

Painting a Picture

William Johnson's best-known art is called folk art. William's pictures showed African Americans in their daily lives. His pictures were bright and colorful, and he used big shapes.

Draw and color or paint a picture about yourself. Use bright colors and big shapes the way William did.

Michael Jordan
Athlete

"... I had achieved everything in basketball I could. And when that happened, I felt it was time to call it a career." The words of Michael Jordan on October 6, 1993, shocked his fans. Could it be true? Michael Jordan, the 30-year-old Chicago Bulls' superstar, was retiring from basketball.

Michael Jordan was a leading scorer in professional basketball. He had led his team to many NBA championships. He had won the Most Valuable Player award three times. He held scoring records in the league. Michael also led basketball's Olympic Dream Team to a gold medal victory in the 1992 Olympics. He appeared to have everything going for him. Why retire?

People asked what he was going to do when he retired. "My father used to say that you never know what you can accomplish until you try," said Michael. He had hinted that he wanted to play baseball with the Chicago White Sox.

After baseball spring training in 1994, Michael was asked to play with the Birmingham Barons. The team was not famous like the White Sox. But there Michael could improve his game. He needed to become a better hitter and fielder. Later he could play with the White Sox. Michael did not mind the step down. Though he was not the best baseball player, he was happy about playing, and his teammates liked him. Many fans came to his games.

Some people could not understand why Michael gave up being a superstar basketball player. He had to start all over at the bottom in baseball. He did not make a lot of money. His fans saw him strike out. Michael said his father always told him, "... it's never too late to do anything you want to do."

More on Michael

Michael Jordan officially ended his retirement from basketball on March 18, 1995. He returned to the Chicago Bulls where he proved once again that he was a basketball superstar.

Name _____ Date _____

What do you remember about Michael Jordan?

Draw a line from the beginning of the sentence in Column A to the correct ending in Column B.

Column A **Column B**

1. Michael was on the Olympic   the Chicago White Sox.

2. The team on which Michael wanted to play baseball is   awards three times.

3. The team on which Michael played baseball is   the Birmingham Barons.

4. Michael has won Most Valuable Player   Dream Team in 1992.

5. Michael left basketball to play   baseball for one year.

More About Michael Jordan

Michael skipped his last year of college to play basketball for the Chicago Bulls. The next two summers he went back to the University of North Carolina. He wanted to finish college. It makes people proud to finish what they start.

Write about something you have started and finished. Were you proud of your work?

_____
_____
_____
_____
_____

Name _____ Date _____

Writing Down the Problems

Michael Jordan scored many points playing basketball for the Chicago Bulls. His Bulls jersey number is 23.

Look at the picture below. There are ten mistakes. Circle and write a number next to each mistake as you find it. Write what was wrong next to the corresponding number below.

1. _____
2. _____
3. _____
4. _____
5. _____
6. _____
7. _____
8. _____
9. _____
10. _____

© Steck-Vaughn Company   55   Famous African Americans 3–4, SV 6791-3

Jackie Joyner-Kersee
Athlete

"Pump your arms, Jackie! This is it!" Al Joyner yelled above the noise of the crowd. Jackie was running the 800-meter race in the 1984 Olympics in Los Angeles, California. Jackie had hurt one of her legs days before, and it was bothering her. Clearly she was in pain. It was slowing her down. She did not seem to have the strength to win the race.

Jackie was competing in the heptathalon, the most difficult women's track and field event. The 800-meter race is one of its seven parts. Jackie's brother, Al, was competing at the Olympics, too. He had already won a gold medal in the triple jump. He knew how hard Jackie had trained. He had to do something to help her.

Al ran inside the track, shouting and urging Jackie not to give up. This was her big chance. Jackie heard Al's voice, and it was the encouragement she needed. She seemed to gain new strength. Running faster, Jackie gained distance on the leader. She finished the race less than two seconds behind the gold-medal winner.

Jackie won a silver medal that day. She knew in her heart she could win a gold medal if she had another chance. Jackie, determined to be the best, trained harder than ever. She represented the United States at the Olympics in 1988, 1992, and 1996. She received five medals in addition to the silver she won in 1984. From her participation in these Olympics, Jackie has earned three gold, one silver, and two bronze Olympic medals. Some people call her the world's greatest woman athlete.

About the Heptathalon

The heptathalon consists of seven parts. They are the 100-meter hurdles, the shot put, the high jump, the 200-meter run, the long jump, the javelin throw, and the 800-meter run. Jackie also competes in the individual long jump event at the Olympic games.

Name _____ Date _____

What do you remember about Jackie Joyner-Kersee?

The six events in the box are from the story about Jackie Joyner-Kersee. Rewrite them in the order that they occurred.

> Jackie finished the race less than 2 seconds behind the gold-medal winner.
> Jackie won the silver medal in the 800-meter race in 1984.
> From inside the track, Al Joyner shouted encouragement to Jackie.
> Jackie had hurt one of her legs.

1. _____

2. _____

3. _____

4. _____

More About Jackie Joyner-Kersee

Pretend you are a writer for a sports magazine. You are going to write about Jackie Joyner-Kersee. To get your story, you will interview Jackie. Write three questions to ask her.

1. _____
2. _____
3. _____

Name _____   Date _____

Reading a Graph

Jackie Joyner-Kersee's favorite track and field event is the long jump. She holds many records in this event. Jackie has been doing the long jump for many years at many different track meets all over the world. Each jump is different.

Below is a graph that shows the length of seven of Jackie's long jumps. Marks are used to show feet and inches. For example, two feet and two inches would look like this: 2'2". The name and year of the track meets are listed, too.

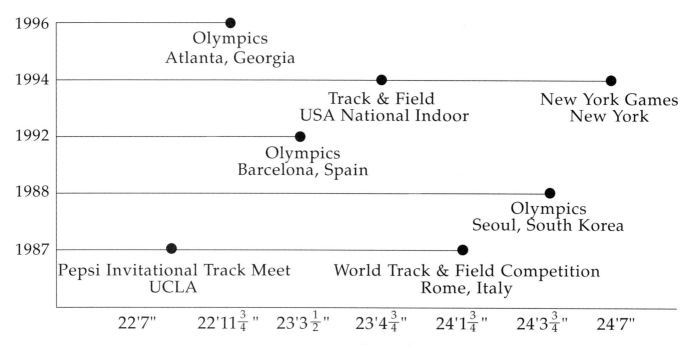

Use the graph to fill in the correct answers to the questions.

1. What is the longest jump Jackie has made? _____

2. How far did Jackie jump in the 1996 Olympics? _____

3. Where was Jackie when she jumped 24'1$\frac{3}{4}$"? _____

4. In what year did Jackie jump 22'7"? _____

Measure Jackie's longest jump. Get your teacher's permission to go into the hallway or outside if you need more room. Use a piece of tape to mark the beginning and end of the jump. Athletes get a running start for the long jump. Even so, can you imagine jumping that far?

Name _____ Date _____

Dr. Martin Luther King, Jr.
Man of Peace

He is the man who made the greatest contribution to the civil rights movement. Thanks to Dr. Martin Luther King, Jr., people of all races now work, play, and study together. But it was not easy to make the changes.

It was hot on August 28, 1963. There were 250,000 people packed into the Washington Plaza. Police were dressed in riot gear. Night sticks were drawn. Face shields were down. Some white people shook their heads. Others shouted at the man about to begin his speech. African-American and white people stood side-by-side to hear this man speak.

"I have a dream," Dr. Martin Luther King, Jr., told the crowd. His voice echoed from the loudspeaker. "I have a dream that my four little children one day will live in a nation where they will not be judged by the color of their skin but by the content of their character." Dr. King spoke out for equality for African Americans. When he finished his speech, the people cheered.

For the next five years, Dr. Martin Luther King, Jr., kept fighting to end segregation. Segregation kept white people and African Americans apart. He led many peaceful marches and gatherings. He worked with world leaders. Millions of people heard him speak. Dr. King and his followers helped get many laws changed.

Dr. King did not live to see his dream come true. But his work helped end segregation in America.

More About Dr. King

Dr. Martin Luther King, Jr., was killed when he was 39 years old. A prisoner who had escaped from jail shot him. Dr. King is buried in Atlanta, his birthplace.

Dr. King won the Nobel Peace Prize in 1964.

Name _____ Date _____

What do you remember about Dr. Martin Luther King, Jr.?

Find the best ending for each sentence. Fill in the circle next to it.

1. Segregation laws
   - ○ a. kept people of different skin colors apart.
   - ○ b. are now laws in the United States.
   - ○ c. were unfair to many people.
   - ○ d. kept people of different skin colors apart and were unfair to many people.

2. Dr. King worked hard for
   - ○ a. the environment.
   - ○ b. civil rights.
   - ○ c. animal rights.
   - ○ d. all of the above

3. Dr. King wanted change to
   - ○ a. be peaceful.
   - ○ b. be hard for white people.
   - ○ c. have a lot of fighting.
   - ○ d. have a lot of fighting and be hard for white people.

4. Dr. King's work made some people
   - ○ a. want to change the unfair laws.
   - ○ b. angry at him.
   - ○ c. very happy.
   - ○ d. all of the above

More About Dr. Martin Luther King, Jr.

These words are carved on Dr. King's tombstone: "Free at last, free at last, thank God Almighty, I'm free at last." What do you think these words mean about Dr. King?

_____

_____

_____

_____

Name _____ Date _____

Making a Time Line

Read about the events in Dr. King's life. Draw a picture in the box next to each event.

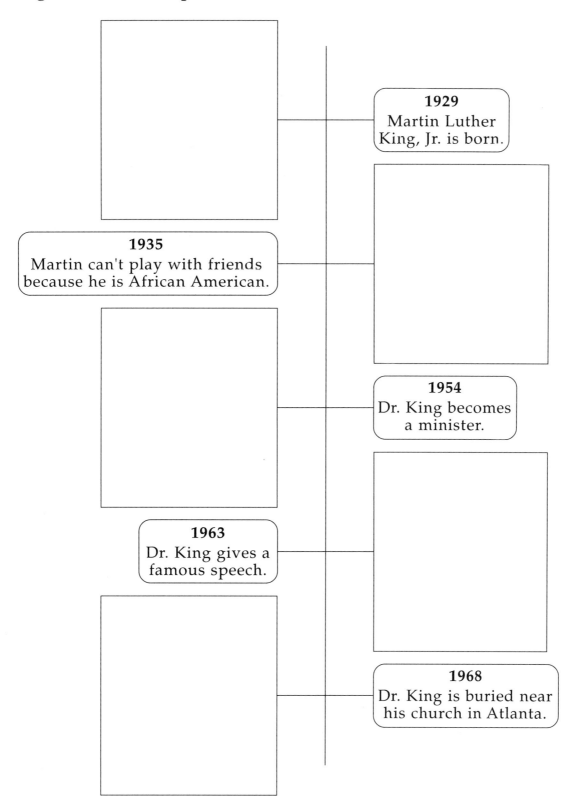

1929
Martin Luther King, Jr. is born.

1935
Martin can't play with friends because he is African American.

1954
Dr. King becomes a minister.

1963
Dr. King gives a famous speech.

1968
Dr. King is buried near his church in Atlanta.

Thurgood Marshall
Supreme Court Justice

Thurgood Marshall passed through the entrance of the United States Supreme Court. Above the doorway were the words "Equal Justice Under Law." He paused to read them and smiled. History would be made today, he thought. The Justices called on the confident African-American lawyer to speak. For years he had planned for this case. He believed strongly in what he had to say. The name of this case was Brown versus the Board of Education of Topeka, Kansas. It was about school segregation.

It was 1954. White children and African-American children did not go to school together. This was the law. Thurgood Marshall didn't think this was fair. Schools for African-American children often had less money than schools for white children. The books and desks were not as good as those of the white students. Thurgood wanted this to change. He felt children of all races should be given the same quality education.

Thurgood began to speak. He was well-prepared. He gave many examples to prove he was right. He said African-American children were not getting an equal education. This was not what the law promised.

The Justices of the Supreme Court all agreed with Thurgood. Not one of them thought he was wrong. Thurgood Marshall won the case. Now children of all races can go to the same schools.

In 1967 President Johnson asked Thurgood Marshall to serve as a Supreme Court Justice. He became the first African American to hold this position. It was a fitting job for a man who had done so much to guarantee "Equal Justice Under Law."

Memorize, Mr. Marshall!

When Thurgood misbehaved in school, his principal sent him to a quiet place to memorize parts of the Constitution. It did not keep him out of trouble, but what he remembered helped him later when he was arguing cases.

Name _____ Date _____

What do you remember about Thurgood Marshall?

Draw a line from the beginning of the sentence in Column A to the correct ending in Column B.

Column A	Column B
1. Thurgood Marshall believed	white and African-American children could not go to the same schools.
2. Segregation meant that	ended segregation in public schools.
3. Thurgood was known for	his fairness.
4. Thurgood Marshall won the court case that	Supreme Court Justice.
5. Thurgood was the first African-American	all children should have an equal education.

More About Thurgood Marshall

Thurgood Marshall was known for his fairness and honesty. Why do you think it is important for a judge to be fair and honest?

_____

_____

_____

_____

Name _____ Date _____

Making Judgments

Thurgood Marshall had to judge, or decide what was fair, when he was in court. Sometimes it is easy to see what is wrong and what is right. Other times it is hard to decide. A judge has to find out as much as he or she can about a problem before a decision, or judgment, can be made.

You be the judge:

Two sisters, Dee and Diana, each had $5.00 on Monday. On Thursday, Dee went to a movie. Diana wanted to go, too, but she did not get to go.

Do you know enough to decide if this is fair for both girls? Circle one:
Yes   No

Here are some more facts about Dee and Diana: Dee saved her money all week. She was saving it for something she really wanted. Diana spent her money on candy and ice cream on Tuesday and Wednesday. She did not think about saving her money.

What do you think now? Is it fair for Dee to go to the movie without Diana? Knowing all the facts can change what you think. Write what you would say to Dee and Diana.

_____
_____
_____
_____
_____

Name _____ Date _____

Toni Morrison
Writer

The winter wind was howling outside Toni Morrison's home in Syracuse, New York. Her two little boys had been tucked into bed. The rest of the evening was hers. At 9:00 Toni Morrison sat down at her writing desk. She was writing a story about a little African-American girl who wanted blue eyes.

The Bluest Eye was a story Toni had written about five years before. She had put the story away and had forgotten about it. In the last few days, Toni had found it again and started writing it as a novel. Toni wanted to do the story for African Americans. She wanted it to be about their culture and lives. She used the familiar sayings of the African-American people. Toni felt no other writer was writing this way. She wanted to try something different.

She thought of her own childhood in Loraine, Ohio. She remembered the African-American girl in Loraine who had wanted blue eyes like white girls. *The Bluest Eye* is about this girl and her friends. After many late nights of writing, Toni finished her book. It was published in 1969 and was well-received by African Americans and white people alike.

Toni has continued writing since she finished *The Bluest Eye*. She has written other books and plays. She won the Pulitzer Prize for her 1987 book called *Beloved*, a story about a woman who escaped from slavery. And in 1993 Toni Morrison received one of the world's highest honors. She became the first African American to win the Nobel Prize in Literature.

Toni's Title

When Toni was in college, no one could pronounce her first name, Chloe. She was so annoyed by this that she changed her name to Toni!

Name _____ Date _____

What do you remember about Toni Morrison?

Underline the word or group of words which completes each sentence correctly.

1. In college Toni Morrison changed her
   a. major.
   b. name.
   c. feelings about people.

2. Toni's writing helps readers
   a. learn to read.
   b. understand African Americans.
   c. learn new languages.

3. Her book *Beloved* won
   a. the Nobel Prize.
   b. the Iron Cross.
   c. the Pulitzer Prize.

4. In 1993 Toni Morrison was awarded _____ for her writings.
   a. the grand prize
   b. the Nobel Prize in Literature
   c. a scholarship

The Nobel Prize

Research the Nobel Prize. Write about it. Identify at least two other people who have received this prize.

_____

_____

_____

_____

_____

Name _____ Date _____

Writing a Story

 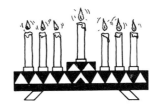

Toni Morrison writes for African Americans. She writes about the African-American way of life. Even though we are all the same in many ways, different cultures have their own special ways of celebrating. The things that make us different from each other are also the things that make us interesting to each other.

Think about something that your family does that you think is special. Maybe it is a tradition that has been passed down from your grandparents and their parents. Write about it. Then draw a picture to go with your story.

_____
_____
_____
_____
_____

Colin Powell
War Hero/Military Adviser

The helicopter was carrying its five passengers over a section of Vietnam, a country in Asia. The pilot wanted to land the helicopter in a small area. As he brought the chopper close to the ground, one of the propellers hit a tree. Suddenly the helicopter crashed to the ground and began to burn. One of the passengers, Major Colin Powell, jumped from the helicopter safely. But what would happen to the other passengers?

After Major Powell had freed himself from the wreckage, he realized that the other three passengers and the pilot were still trapped inside. In spite of the smoke and danger, he returned to the helicopter four times to rescue them all. As he helped the last man out, the helicopter burst into flames.

For his brave actions, Major Powell received a Soldier's Medal. But this was just one of many honors and medals that Colin Powell would receive during his career in the Army. He would hold the highest military position in the United States. In 1989 Colin Powell became Chairman of the Joint Chiefs of Staff. He was 52 years old. This made him the youngest man in history to hold this position.

Colin Powell has fought bravely for his country in wars, lead troops in battles, advised Presidents, and worked with other leaders to avoid trouble. He even thought about running for President in 1996. He has been a great leader and a role model to United States citizens.

Think About This!

Colin went to North Carolina when he first joined the Army. North Carolina was not like New York, his home. In North Carolina, he couldn't even order a hamburger at a drive-in. African Americans had to go to the back door for their food.

Name _____ Date _____

What do you remember about Colin Powell?

Fill in each blank with the correct word. Select your answers from the word box. You will not use all the words.

military   Soldier's   advice   trouble   bravery   Joint   army

1. Colin Powell won a _____ Medal for saving the people in the helicopter.

2. Colin Powell will be remembered for his _____.

3. Colin Powell was asked by United States Presidents for his

   _____.

4. The Chairman of the Joint Chiefs of Staff is the highest

   _____ position in the United States.

5. Colin has helped the United States avoid _____

   with other countries.

More About Colin Powell

Colin Powell is a hero. He has done many brave things. He was given the Purple Heart for being hurt in war. Have you ever needed to be brave? Write about a brave thing that you or someone you know has done.

_____

_____

_____

Name _____ Date _____

Finding the Mistakes

General Colin Powell joined the Army when he finished college. In the Army people wear special uniforms. Their uniforms must be kept clean and in good condition.

There are two pictures of Colin Powell in Army uniform below. The one on the left side of the page is correct. The one on the right side of the page has many things wrong with it. Compare the two pictures. Find the 12 mistakes. Number them as you find them.

© Steck-Vaughn Company   70   Famous African Americans 3-4, SV 6791-3

Leontyne Price
Opera Singer

The audience sat spellbound. The stage was set for an Italian opera. The actors all sang their parts. But one stood out from the rest. The singer who was playing the part of Leonora had a voice that was captivating. It would even be called perfect.

When she finished singing, the audience rose to its feet. They began to clap. The Metropolitan Opera House in New York was quiet again 42 minutes later. The singer had just received the longest ovation in the history of the opera company.

That singer was Leontyne Price. She had been singing since she was just two years old. Her parents, her teachers, and her friends in Mississippi had all helped her to get the training and education she would need to be a success. Years of practice had brought her to where she was that day.

In 1964 President Johnson awarded Leontyne the Freedom Medal. This is the highest honor a citizen of the United States can receive. President Johnson said, "Her singing has brought light to her land."

Leontyne loves singing. She says, "You must like what you are doing if you want to be happy and successful." This is a good thing to remember, coming from the woman with "the golden voice."

More About Leontyne Price

Leontyne's parents traded one of their nicest things, their Victrola, a record player, so that Leontyne could practice on a real piano. Before that Leontyne had been practicing on a toy piano!

Name _____ Date _____

What do you remember about Leontyne Price?

Use the words in the word box to answer the questions. Write your answers in the boxes and circles under each question. (You will not use all the words from the word box.)

Match the numbered circles with the circles in Question 6 to find the answer.

| Mississippi | piano | ovation | Freedom | singer |
| golden | Alabama | actress | pretty | |

1. Leontyne got a 42-minute ☐☐◯☐☐☐.
                                            5

2. President Johnson awarded Leontyne the ☐☐☐☐☐◯☐ Medal.
                                                               1

3. Leontyne was a famous ☐☐☐☐☐◯.
                                   4

4. Leontyne grew up in ☐☐☐☐☐☐☐◯☐☐.
                                         2

5. Leontyne has been called the woman with the ☐☐☐☐◯☐ voice.
                                                                              3

6. What kind of singing made Leontyne famous? ◯◯◯◯◯
                                                                                                       1 2 3 4 5

More About Leontyne Price

Leontyne sang opera. An opera is like a play, but the actors sing all their lines. Have you ever heard an opera? Find the name of an opera. Write it here.

_____

What kind of music do you like? Write what you like and why.

_____

_____

© Steck-Vaughn Company   72   Famous African Americans 3-4, SV 6791-3

Name _____ Date _____

Listening to Sound Waves

Music was a big part of Leontyne Price's life. You can make some musical sounds with some glasses of water and a spoon.

Fill several glasses with different amounts of water. Gently tap the glasses with your spoon.

What do you hear? _____

Do all the glasses have the same sound? _____

Can you guess why the sounds are different?

_____

_____

When you tap one of the glasses, you hear a sound. This sound comes from sound waves. The sound waves travel through the water and to your ear. The longer the sound wave travels, or the more water in the glass, the lower the sound will be. The shorter the sound wave travels, or the less water in the glass, the higher the sound will be. (See the drawing below.)

Tap your glasses again, and listen carefully to each sound. Arrange your glasses from the lowest note to the highest. Try to play a tune, like *Do Re Mi (Doe, a Deer)*, or *Mary Had a Little Lamb*. If your glasses are different sizes, you may need to adjust the water levels so that you will have several notes to play.

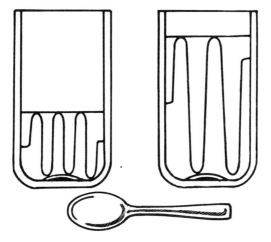

Name _____ Date _____

David Robinson
Scholar/Athlete

In 1984 a young man named David Robinson was graduating from high school in Florida. He had been a star player on his high school basketball team, and college scouts had been watching him. Many colleges wanted David to come and play basketball for them. But David had decided that he would attend Annapolis, a naval academy in Maryland. At Annapolis David would be trained to become an officer in the United States Navy.

David studied computer science at Annapolis. He continued to play basketball. He also continued to grow. David grew six more inches in college, to a height of 7'1"! The basketball world had not forgotten about David. They had watched him play and grow at Annapolis. The NBA selected David first in the 1987 draft. But David had made a promise to the Navy. Though he really did want to play basketball, he wanted to do the right thing and keep his promise. He would stay at school for the full five-year term.

But sometimes life has a way of working things out for us. Because of David's height, the officials at Annapolis knew that he would not be able to work on the Navy's submarines or ships, nor would he be able to fly the Navy's planes. They allowed David to leave Annapolis early, shortening his service from five years to two.

Many teams wanted David to play for them. He elected to play for the San Antonio Spurs. Basketball fans had been waiting for years to see David play. They were not disappointed. David was chosen as the best new player in the league in 1987. He continues to be a star basketball player.

Drop David?!!

David Robinson quit his high school basketball team when he was 14. He was afraid he would be dropped from the team!

Name _____ Date _____

What do you remember about David Robinson?

First, read each of the following sentences. Then, write *1st* in the space before the sentence that tells what happened first in David's life. Write *2nd* before the sentence that tells what happened next. Keep going with *3rd*, *4th*, and *5th*.

_____ David decides to stay in college at Annapolis.

_____ David is chosen as the best new player in basketball.

_____ David grows to be 7'1" tall.

_____ David decides to play basketball for the San Antonio Spurs.

_____ David studies math and computer science at the Naval Academy.

More About David Robinson

David Robinson grew to be 7'1" tall. He was too tall for the Navy's airplanes and ships. But being tall helped him to be a better basketball player.

Can you think of two other jobs where being tall might be helpful? Name the jobs, and write why.

1. _____

2. _____

Can you think of two jobs where being short might be better? Name the jobs, and write why.

1. _____

2. _____

Name _____ Date _____

Breaking the Code

The college David Robinson attended has the same name as the town where it is. This town is also the capital of the state of Maryland.

Each space for the name of David's school has a picture below it. Find the letter that begins the name of each picture, and write it in the blank. Continue until all the blanks are filled.

How many other state capitals do you know? List five states other than Maryland, and name the capital of each.

State	Capital

© Steck-Vaughn Company
Famous African Americans 3-4, SV 6791-3

Wilma Rudolph
Olympic Gold Medalist

Over 40,000 people lined the streets of Clarksville, Tennessee. "Look, here she comes!" one girl cried. "Wilma, we're proud of you!" a man yelled out. The crowd screamed and cheered as Wilma Rudolph passed. Nearly everyone in her hometown had turned out for this parade in her honor.

The year was 1960. Wilma Rudolph, now a hero, had just returned from the Olympics in Rome, Italy. There she had become the first woman to win three gold medals at an Olympics. She won first place in both the 200- and the 100-meter races. She also placed first with her teammates in the relay race.

At the parade friends and neighbors thought about Wilma's childhood. They had watched her struggle to walk. She had had polio and had worn a metal leg brace. They remembered her talent in basketball. They remembered also her speed on the track. She had never lost a race in high school. They recalled proudly the running star she became in college. All of that had prepared Wilma for the Olympics.

Wilma smiled and waved as she saw her friends and neighbors. She was a true champion. Her first steps in life had been slow. But she had set a goal for herself. She had worked hard when it was painful to do so. Wilma Rudolph overcame her handicap and became an Olympic hero.

Getting it Together

The parade for Wilma was the first event for both white and African-American people in Clarksville, Tennessee.

Name _____ Date _____

What do you remember about Wilma Rudolph?

Fill in each blank with the correct word or words. Select your answers from the word box. You will not use all the words.

| basketball | track | Italy | three |
| five | race | illness | tennis |

1. A serious childhood _____ left Wilma unable to walk.

2. Before she began running, Wilma played _____ .

3. Wilma was a _____ star in college.

4. Wilma never lost a _____ in high school.

5. The 1960 Olympics were in _____ .

6. Wilma Rudolph won _____ gold medals for running.

More About Wilma Rudolph

Wilma Rudolph was named "Female Athlete of the Year" in 1960. Write why you think she was given this award.

_____
_____
_____
_____

Awarding Gold Medals

Gold medals are awarded to people who are the best at a sport. Think of three of your friends who do something well. Make a medal for each friend. Be sure to write the person's name and why the person is getting the medal. Present the medals to your friends.

Harriet Tubman
Champion of Freedom

Harriet Tubman didn't move. Her eyes darted in the darkness. Her heart was beating fast. She had heard the sounds of horses and men. She knew what that meant—slave catchers. She had warned the other slaves with her that this could happen. If they were caught, they could be returned to their owners. Or they could be killed. They knew the risks.

This was Maryland in the 1850s. Helping slaves escape to freedom was dangerous. Harriet knew this well. She helped many slaves escape. So far she had not been caught. Would the slave catchers get her this time? Harriet knew there was a reward out for her arrest. The person who brought her in would get $40,000.

Harriet Tubman worked with the Underground Railroad. It wasn't really a train. Instead, it was a group of people who helped slaves escape to freedom. Harriet was famous. She knew all the tricks. She memorized where to find the safe places to hide. Now she needed to get to the next stop. Her friends were there and would help.

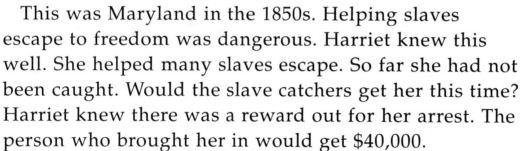

Harriet and the group of escaped slaves waited without moving for a long time. The darkness of the night was fading. Finally, human voices and the sounds of animals could no longer be heard. The slave catchers were gone, and it was safe to continue. Harriet Tubman had many frightening nights like this one. She risked her own life many times to help other slaves. She was a true hero.

Amazing Mrs. Tubman

In all, Harriet Tubman helped over 300 slaves escape to freedom. Over a ten-year period, she returned to the slave states about 20 times. She was never captured.

Name _____ Date _____

What do you remember about Harriet Tubman?

The following sentences are false. Rewrite them so that they will be true.

1. Freedom was not important to Harriet Tubman.

   _____

2. The Underground Railroad was a train.

   _____

3. It was easy for Harriet to help slaves escape.

   _____

4. Harriet Tubman helped about 20 slaves escape to freedom.

   _____

5. Harriet Tubman was found by slave catchers twice.

   _____

More About Harriet Tubman

Harriet Tubman was a strong-willed person. Some people called her stubborn. What words would people use to describe you? Write four of them. Ask a friend to write four words to describe you, too. Compare your lists.

1. _____   3. _____

2. _____   4. _____

Name _____ Date _____

Finding Your Way

Harriet helped over 300 slaves escape to freedom. The route they took went from the South to the North. They had to be careful not to get caught.

Take Harriet through the maze as she travels from a plantation in the South to Ohio, a state in the North where slaves could become free. Then answer the questions below using the compass rose.

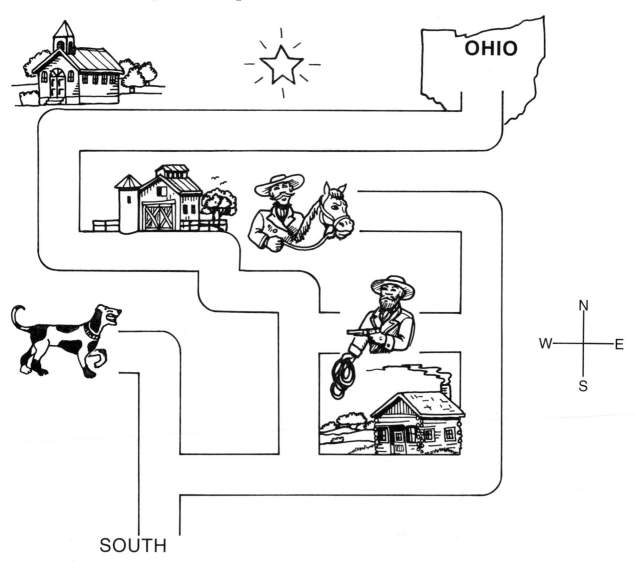

1. In which direction did Harriet travel to get to Ohio? _____

2. Name something that is east of the dog. _____

3. If you left the church and headed south, at what place would you arrive first?

_____

Booker T. Washington
Educator

On the platform stood the President of the United States. On one side of him was the governor of Alabama. Both of these men were white. On the other side of President McKinley was a man who had been born a slave. His name was Booker T. Washington. This scene was very unusual for the time, December 16, 1899. Elected officials who were white did not often meet with African Americans.

The President and the governor were there at Booker's invitation. They had come to see the great works he had accomplished at Tuskegee Normal and Industrial Institute in Alabama. The Institute was a school for African Americans.

Booker watched with pride as the students of Tuskegee passed in front of the President and honored guests. He remembered the time 20 years ago when he first came to the Institute. The only buildings he had for his school were a broken-down shack and an old hen house. He had owned no property, and Booker had been the only teacher. Now there were 66 buildings, and the school owned 2,300 acres of land!

Students who attended Tuskegee were taught useful jobs like teaching and farming. Booker was very proud that white people and African Americans wanted his students to work for them. His only concern was that he could not graduate enough students to meet the demand.

The President gave a speech. He praised Booker as one of the great leaders of African Americans. He was respected in the United States and abroad as a skilled educator and a great speaker. It was a fine day in the history of Tuskegee Normal and Industrial Institute.

Booker's School

George Washington Carver, another famous African American, did his great work to help the southern farmers at Tuskegee.

Name _____ Date _____

What do you remember about Booker T. Washington?

Choose the word or words that complete each sentence correctly. Circle the letter.

1. Presidents _____ met with African Americans in 1899.
   a. never
   b. rarely
   c. often

2. Booker began his school with only _____ buildings.
   a. five
   b. three
   c. two

3. Booker's school was the _____.
   a. Tuskegee Normal and Industrial Institute
   b. University of Alabama
   c. Hampton Institute

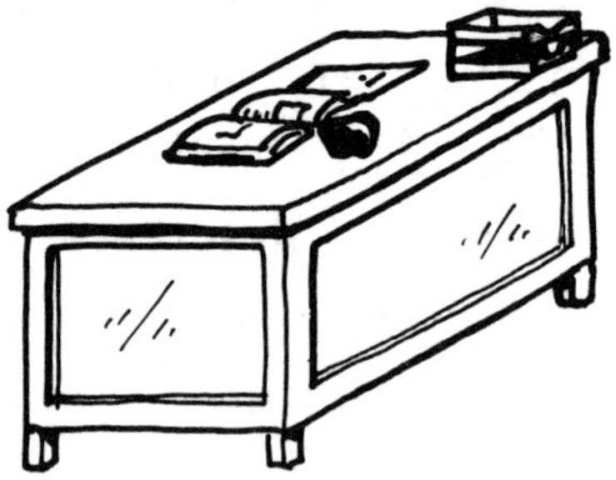

4. At Tuskegee Institute, Booker wanted to train students _____.
   a. to speak French
   b. to do useful jobs like teaching and farming
   c. to work on cars

5. Many people wanted _____ to work for them.
   a. Booker
   b. Booker's students
   c. white students

More About Booker T. Washington

Some of the things the students at Tuskegee Institute could learn were farming, carpentry, and masonry. Choose the one that you might like to learn. Write what you could do if you learned it.

I would like to learn _____.

Then I would be able to _____

_____

_____.

Name _____ Date _____

Writing Directions

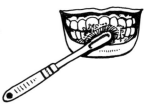

Booker T. Washington was an educator. Teachers have to be good at explaining things. They have to give good, clear directions. Do you think you could teach someone?

Look at the three choices in the box. Circle one, and write the directions for how to do it. Be careful not to leave out any steps. Later you and a partner can try to follow each other's directions. (You may not need all ten steps, or you may need more.)

1. making a peanut butter sandwich
2. brushing your teeth
3. making a bed

Steps:

1. _____
2. _____
3. _____
4. _____
5. _____
6. _____
7. _____
8. _____
9. _____
10. _____

Denzel Washington
Actor

A crowd has gathered in the Audubon Ballroom in New York City. It is February 21, 1965. Outside it is icy cold. Inside the people are warm. They are waiting to see Malcolm X. They are his followers. Malcolm X's speeches are full of fire. His ideas are exciting. The people are anxious to hear what he has to say today.

Suddenly someone fires a gun. Malcolm X falls to the floor, dead. Security guards jump up and return fire. People begin screaming and running in every direction.

"Cut! That's a wrap!" calls Spike Lee, the director. The camera men stop their cameras. The crowd begins to leave the set. Denzel Washington gets to his feet. He takes off the glasses he has been wearing. They are a part of his costume that helps him look like Malcolm X. He wipes his face with a cloth. Making the movie has been exciting and fun. But it is also hard work to act like someone else and do a good job of it!

Denzel Washington is now a well-known actor. But growing up in Mt. Vernon, New York, he did not know what he wanted to be. Being part of a children's play one day, he found he was good at acting. He had had fun doing it, too. That's when he began studying to be an actor.

Denzel has been in more than 20 movies. Some of them, besides *Malcolm X*, are *Glory*, *Crimson Tide*, and *Courage Under Fire*. His talent and hard work have made him one of the most famous African-American actors.

One More Thing!

Denzel Washington feels he owes a lot to the Boys & Girls Club of America. He was a member of the club for most of his childhood. The people there gave him support. They encouraged him to make the most of his life.

Name _____ Date _____

What do you remember about Denzel Washington?

The following sentences are false. Write them so that they will be true.

1. Malcolm X is really Denzel Washington.

_____

2. Acting is fun and easy.

_____

3. Denzel Washington has been in a couple of movies.

_____

4. Denzel would rather not be an actor.

_____

5. The Boys & Girls Club of America did not do much for Denzel Washington.

_____

More About Denzel

Denzel has been in many movies. He has acted happy, sad, brave, frightened, and angry. He makes us believe that he really feels the way he is acting. Think of a way that you could act to make people believe you are sad or happy or afraid. Try it with a friend, and see if your friend can guess how you are acting.

Name _____ Date _____

Making a Pictograph

Actors like Denzel have to act in many ways. They show us how they feel by the expressions on their faces. We all use our faces to show how we feel. Sometimes we don't even know it!

Get a magazine. Cut out as many different faces as you can find. See if you can put them in groups of expressions. Are some happy? Are they sad? Do they look angry or afraid? After you have grouped them, paste them onto your pictograph in a line. Go from left to right on the page.

Happy
Sad
Angry
Afraid
Others

Which group on your graph has the most faces? _____

Daniel Hale Williams
Surgeon

It is the year 1893. In Chicago a man is admitted to Provident Hospital. He has a knife wound in his chest. It is very close to his heart. No doctor has ever been able to save such a patient. But this patient, James Cornish, is a very lucky man. He is about to become the first man to live through heart surgery.

Dr. Daniel Hale Williams makes a bigger cut in James's chest. He takes out part of a rib bone so that he can see the damage. Then he goes to work repairing the wound. Dr. Williams closes the opening in James's chest to complete the operation.

For the next four days, James Cornish's life is still in danger. His temperature is high. His heartbeat is not normal. Then his health begins to improve. Two months after entering the hospital, James is fully recovered. Though he has come close to dying, he leaves with only a scar.

When other doctors heard about Dr. Williams' success, they were amazed. Sadly, many didn't believe that an African American could have done such an astonishing thing. Dr. Williams did not care what people thought. He continued his work as always.

Today Dr. Daniel Hale Williams is remembered as a brilliant surgeon and a pioneer in open heart surgery.

Dr. Williams Did More

Dr. Daniel Hale Williams is also remembered for his work in building hospitals and training schools for African-American doctors and nurses. During his time most hospitals did not hire African-American doctors and nurses. Nor did they treat African-American patients.

Name _____ Date _____

What do you remember about Daniel Hale Williams?

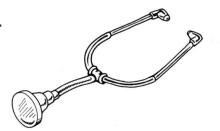

Read the sentences. Circle the word or words below that make a true sentence. Write the words in the blanks.

1. Daniel Hale Williams helped many African-American _____ .

   teachers　　　　**singers**　　　　**doctors and nurses**

2. Some doctors did not believe Dr. Williams because he was _____ .

   African American　　**young**　　　　**not trained**

3. _____ Hospital is where Dr. Williams did his famous surgery.

   Chicago　　　　**Miami Medical**　　　　**Provident**

4. Dr. Williams was the first doctor to successfully operate on a person's _____ .

   eyes　　　　**heart**　　　　**legs**

5. Dr. Williams raised money to build _____ .

   hospitals　　　　**zoos**　　　　**museums**

More About Daniel Hale Williams

Dr. Williams was the first doctor to operate on a human heart and save his patient's life. Pretend you are the patient he saved. What would you say to Dr. Williams?

_____

_____

Name _____ Date _____

Labeling the Circulatory System

Dr. Williams knew much about the human body. Below is a drawing of a person that shows the circulatory system. All people have several systems in their bodies. The circulatory system is one of these.

The circulatory system carries blood throughout the body. It is made up mainly of blood vessels and a pumping organ, the heart. It supplies the cells of the body with food and oxygen and takes away the wastes.

Each of the parts of the circulatory system listed in the box has a letter beside it. Match the letter of each part with the letters around the body in the picture. Write the name of each part on the correct line. Find the places on your own body where these parts would be found.

a. heart
b. lungs
c. arteries
d. veins

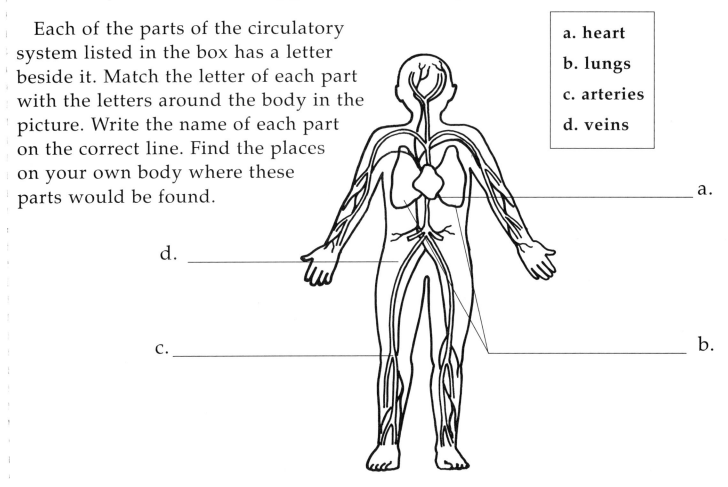

d. _____

c. _____

a. _____

b. _____

Name five other systems in the human body.

_____   _____

_____   _____

_____

Bonus: Name as many organs within each system as you can.

Name _____ Date _____

Tiger Woods
Golfer / U.S. Amateur Champion

The cameras watched. Sports fans watched and wondered. Could this young golfer do what no one had ever done?

On a hot August day in Oregon, 1996, Eldrick "Tiger" Woods faced history. Two years before, he became the first African American to win the men's U.S. Amateur golf title. He won again in 1995. No one had ever won three straight titles. Tiger had already beaten five other golfers that week. Now he faced his last test.

Steve Scott won his first five golf matches that week, too. Steve and Tiger were the last two players. One would win. One would lose.

Early in the match, Steve Scott jumped out to a big lead. But Tiger didn't panic. He stayed calm. Slowly he fought back. By the last hole of the day, Tiger had come back to tie. "Against Tiger Woods, no lead is safe," said Steve. The match was now even. This meant that Steve and Tiger had to play to sudden death. In sudden death the first person to win a hole wins the tournament.

They tied the first extra hole. On the second hole, Tiger needed only to make a one-foot putt to win. When his golf ball landed in the bottom of the cup, the young man from Cypress, California, had made history…again.

Tiger Woods won his third U. S. Amateur golf title in a row. And he was only twenty years old!

Tiger Woods' Firsts

1st to win three U.S. Junior Amateur golf titles

———

1st to win both the Junior Amateur and the U.S. Amateur titles

———

1st African American to win a U.S. Amateur title

———

1st to win three U.S. Amateur titles in a row

© Steck-Vaughn Company

92

Famous African Americans 3-4, SV 6791-3

Name _____ Date _____

What do you remember about Tiger Woods?

Choose the answer to each question from the word box. Write it in the blank.

Steve Scott	eleven	golf	
Sam	Eldrick	Ohio	
Oregon	California	an eagle	a one-foot putt
twenty	tennis	Maine	Jack Nicklaus

1. Tiger Woods has made a name for himself in what sport?

   _____

2. What is Tiger's first name?

   _____

3. Who was Tiger's opponent when he won his third U.S. Amateur golf title?

   _____

4. How old was Tiger when he won his third U.S. Amateur golf title?

   _____

5. In what state were Tiger and Steve playing in 1996?

   _____

6. In what state does Tiger Woods live?

   _____

7. What kind of shot did Tiger have to make to win his 1996 Amateur golf title?

   _____

More About Tiger Woods

Tiger Woods is an African American. There are some golf courses, even today, that have rules to keep African Americans from golfing there. What do you think about these rules?

_____

_____

Name _____ Date _____

Teeing Off

Fit the following words into the crossword puzzle. (Hint: Match the number of spaces and the number of letters in each word to solve the puzzle.)

- autograph
- caddie
- hole
- amateur
- drive
- cup
- country club

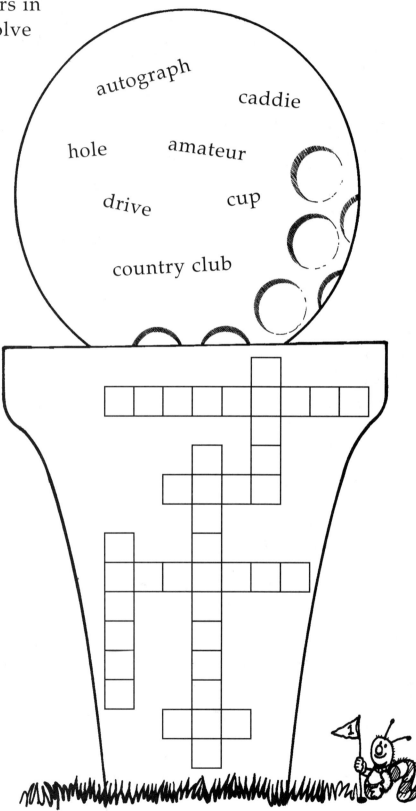

94

ANSWER KEY

pp. 6–7 Assessment: 1. b 2. c 3. a 4. c 5. b 6. a 7. b 8. a 9. c. 10. b 11. George Washington Carver 12. Any 2: shot put, high jump, 100-meter hurdles, 200-meter run, long jump, javelin throw, 800-meter run 13. a parade to honor Wilma Rudolph 14. saving blood 15. running or track 16. She wrote in the way that African Americans speak. 17. He was too tall to fit into the Navy's airplanes and ships. 18. Harriet had to watch out for the slave catchers and their dogs. She and the slaves she was helping could be caught, punished, and killed for trying to escape.

p. 8 Answers will vary.

p. 9 Answers will vary.

p. 10 Answers will vary.

p. 11 Answers will vary.

p. 12 1. Combinations of: Indiana, Illinois, Ohio, Pennsylvania, New York, Michigan, Wisconsin; (not as good, but possible: Vermont, New Hampshire, and Maine) 2. Atlantic Ocean 3. Three of any: Iowa, Illinois, Michigan, Indiana, Ohio, Philadelphia, New York, New Jersey, Massachusetts, Vermont, New Hampshire

p. 15 1. b 2. c 3. b 4. a 5. b

p. 16 Answers will vary.

p. 18 1. true 2. false 3. false 4. ? 5. true 6. false 7. true MORE ABOUT: Answers will vary.

p. 19 Students should circle: away, day, too, do, chores, doors.
WRITING A POEM: Answers will vary.

p. 21 1. b 2. d 3. c 4. c MORE ABOUT: Answers will vary.

p. 24 1. musician 2. soul 3. 500 4. world 5. unable to see
MORE ABOUT: Answers will vary.

p. 27 1. c 2. b 3. c 4. a 5. a MORE ABOUT: Answers will vary.

p. 30 1. National City, California 2. run, practice 3. 100-meter dash, hurdles
4. 1992 5. Atlanta, Georgia MORE ABOUT: Answers will vary.

p. 33 SENTENCE ORDER: 2, 4, 1, 3, 5. MORE ABOUT: Answers will vary.

p. 36 1. Charles Drew was a well-known doctor. 2. true 3. The Red Cross Blood Bank used Dr. Drew's system, or The Red Cross Blood Bank did not keep Dr. Drew's money. 4. Dr. Drew's system for storing blood is still used today. 5. true
MORE ABOUT: Answers will vary.

p. 37 USING A GRAPH: 1. Answers will vary. 2. N/A
3. Answers will vary. MEASURING: 1. N/A 2. 2 3. 2 4. 4 5. 4 6. N/A 7. Probably more.

p. 39 1. a 2. c 3. c 4. a 5. b MORE ABOUT: Answers will vary.

p. 40 Answers will vary.

p. 42 1. c 2. c 3. a 4. b 5. a MORE ABOUT: Answers will vary.

p. 43 Answers will vary.

p. 45 1. New Jersey 2. The Bodyguard 3. contract 4. music 5. family
MORE ABOUT: Answers will vary.

p. 46 Song Number One: The Greatest Love of All;
Song Number Two: I Will Always Love You

p. 48 1. runner 2. shoes 3. 200 4. 200 5. fastest MORE ABOUT: Answers will vary.

p. 49 Answers will vary.

p. 51 1. false 2. false 3. true 4. true 5. false 6. true 7. false MORE ABOUT: Answers will vary.

ANSWER KEY

p. 54 1. Michael was on the Olympic Dream Team in 1992. 2. The team on which Michael wanted to play baseball is the Chicago White Sox. 3. The team on which Michael played baseball is the Birmingham Barons. 4. Michael has won Most Valuable Player awards three times. 5. Michael left basketball to play baseball for one year.
MORE ABOUT: Answers will vary.

p. 55 In any order: jersey number wrong, team name wrong, hockey stick, football, sock, athletic shoe missing laces & untied, eyebrow missing, one sleeve short, tennis net, beard

p. 57 SENTENCE ORDER: 3, 4, 2, 1 MORE ABOUT: Answers will vary.

p. 58 GRAPH: 1. 24' 7" 2. 22' 11 3/4" 3. 1987 World Track and Field Competition, Rome, Italy 4. 1987

p. 60 1. d 2. b 3. a 4. d MORE ABOUT: Answers will vary.

p. 63 1. Thurgood Marshall believed all children should have an equal education. 2. Segregation meant that white and African-American children could not go to the same schools. 3. Thurgood was known for his fairness. 4. Thurgood Marshall won the court case that ended segregation in public schools. 5. Thurgood was the first African-American Supreme Court Justice. MORE ABOUT: Answers will vary.

p. 64 Answers will vary.

p. 66 1. b 2. b. 3. c 4. b NOBEL PRIZE: Answers will vary.

p. 69 1. Soldier's 2. bravery 3. advice 4. military 5. trouble
MORE ABOUT: Answers will vary.

p. 70 1. AIR FORCE 2. cap 3. jacket 4. happy face 5. Smith 6. MP 7. hammer 8. baseball glove 9. cowboy boot 10. athletic shoe 11. pants 12. shirt and tie

p. 72 1. ovation 2. Freedom 3. singer 4. Mississippi 5. golden 6. opera
MORE ABOUT: Answers will vary.

p. 73 Answers will vary.

p. 75 SENTENCE ORDER: 3rd, 5th, 2nd, 4th, 1st MORE ABOUT: Answers will vary.

p. 76 Annapolis STATE CAPITALS: Answers will vary.

p. 78 1. illness 2. basketball 3. track 4. race 5. Italy 6. three MORE ABOUT: Answers will vary.

p. 81 Close to the following: 1. Freedom was very important to Harriet Tubman 2. The Underground Railroad was not a train. 3. It was not easy [dangerous] for Harriet to help slaves escape. 4. Harriet Tubman helped over 300 slaves escape to freedom. 5. Harriet Tubman was never found by slave catchers.
MORE ABOUT: Answers will vary.

p. 82 1. north 2. slave catcher or cabin 3. farm

p. 84 1. b 2. c 3. a 4. b 5. b MORE ABOUT: Answers will vary.

p. 85 Answers will vary.

p. 87 1. Denzel Washington played Malcolm X. 2. Acting is hard work. 3. Denzel Washington has been in more than 20 movies. 4. Denzel likes being an actor. 5. The Boys & Girls Club of America did much for Denzel Washington.
MORE ABOUT: Answers will vary.

p. 90 1. doctors and nurses 2. African American 3. Provident 4. heart 5. hospitals
MORE ABOUT: Answers will vary.

p. 91 a. heart b. lungs c. arteries d. veins FIVE OTHER SYSTEMS: Any five of these: circulatory, digestive, endocrine, excretory, integumentary, muscular, nervous, reproductive, respiratory, skeletal   BONUS: Answers will vary.

p. 93 1. golf 2. Eldrick 3. Steve Scott 4. twenty 5. Oregon 6. California 7. a one-foot putt MORE ABOUT: Answers will vary.

p. 94 Words as they fit